THE INDUSTRIAL REVOLUTION'S WORKERS AND THEIR LIVES

LUCENT LIBRARY *of* HISTORICAL ERAS

THE INDUSTRIAL REVOLUTION'S WORKERS AND THEIR LIVES

DON NARDO

LUCENT BOOKS
A part of Gale, Cengage Learning

GALE
CENGAGE Learning™

Detroit • New York • San Francisco • New Haven, Conn • Waterville, Maine • London

GALE
CENGAGE Learning

LIBRARY OF CONGRESS CATALOGING-IN-PUBLICATION DATA

Nardo, Don, 1947-
  The industrial revolution's workers and their lives / Don Nardo.
      p. cm. -- (The Lucent library of historical eras)
  Includes bibliographical references and index.
  ISBN 978-1-4205-0154-4 (hbk.)
  1. Industrial revolution--Juvenile literature. 2. Working class--History--
Juvenile literature. 3. Labor--History--Juvenile literature. I. Title.
  HD2321.N374 2009
  331.09'034--dc22

                                                            2009008832

Lucent Books
27500 Drake Rd.
Farmington Hills, MI 48331

ISBN-13: 978-1-4205-0154-4
ISBN-10: 1-4205-0154-2

Printed in the United States of America
1 2 3 4 5 6 7 13 12 11 10 09

Contents

Foreword

Looking back from the vantage point of the present, history can be viewed as a myriad of intertwining roads paved by human events. Some paths stand out—broad highways whose mileposts, even from a distance of centuries, are clear. The events that propelled the rise to power of Germany's Third Reich, its role in World War II, and its eventual demise, for example, are well defined and documented.

Other roads are less distinct, their route sometimes hidden from view. Modern legislatures may have developed from old tribal councils, for example, but the links between them are indistinct in places, open to discussion and interpretation.

The architecture of civilization—law, religion, art, science, and government—as well as the more everyday aspects of our culture—what we eat, what we wear—all developed along the historical roads and byways. In that progression can be traced every facet of modern life.

A broad look back along these roads reveals that many paths—though of vastly different character—seem to converge at a few critical junctions. These intersections are those great historical eras that echo over the long, steady course of human history, extending beyond the past and into the present.

These epic periods of time are the focus of Historical Eras. They shine through the mists of history like beacons, illuminated by a burst of creativity that propels events forward—so bright that we, from thousands of years away, can clearly see the chain of events leading to the present.

Each Historical Eras consists of a set of books that highlight various aspects of these major eras. For example, the Elizabethan England library features volumes on Queen Elizabeth I and her court, Elizabethan theater, the great playwrights, and everyday life in Elizabethan London.

The mini-library approach allows for the division of each era into its most significant and most interesting parts and the exploration of those parts in depth. Also, social and cultural trends as well as illustrative documents and eyewitness accounts can be prominently featured in individual volumes.

Historical Eras presents a wealth of information to young readers. The lively narrative, fully documented primary and secondary source quotations, maps, photographs, sidebars, and annotated bibliographies serve as launching points for class discussion and further research.

In studying the great historical eras, students also develop a better understanding of our own times. What we learn from the past and how we apply it in the present may shape the future and may determine whether our era will be a guiding light to those traveling future roads.

LIFE BEFORE THE INDUSTRIAL REVOLUTION

The Industrial Revolution began in Britain in the mid-1700s and spread to the United States and other lands in the century and a half that followed. It is sometimes called "the machine age" because it witnessed the invention of all manner of complex machines. These were applied to various societal niches, but especially to industry.

The coming of machines spawned an enormous and phenomenally productive factory system in developing nations like Britain, the United States, and France. And it greatly expanded their manufacturing bases, trade relations, and economies. In turn, these few emerging economic giants became influential and militarily powerful and came to dominate most of the globe's smaller, nonindustrialized countries.

In addition to these large-scale national and global alterations, the machine age created a host of smaller-scale changes in the rapidly industrializing societies. In particular, everyday living and working conditions in these societies underwent profound transformations. Before the coming of machines, the pace of life was extremely slow in comparison to the hustle and bustle of the present modern age. The rate of change was slow, too. Over the course of many centuries there had been little scientific and technological advancement. And people had become used to long-standing, traditional farming, home-building, manufacturing, and transportation methods. Society and the customs of everyday life remained largely the same from one generation to the next. To fully appreciate how significantly life changed as a result of industrialization, one must first comprehend the major institutions and rhythms of preindustrial life in Europe and elsewhere.

Working the Land

Unlike today, the chief institution of pre-industrial life was agriculture. Indeed, more than 90 percent of the people dwelled in rural areas (the countryside) and made their livings by farming. Most of these farmers were poor or, at best, of modest means. They grew their own food. And although some owned their own plots of land, many worked on large estates owned by wealthy individuals. It was typical for these peasants to pay their landlords rent, often in the form of crops and livestock.

Of those workers who toiled on the wealthy estates, many in Europe and elsewhere were what are today termed *serfs*. Such individuals were technically free and could not be bought and sold like slaves. However, they were extremely dependent on the landowners for most aspects of their existence and were rarely able to move elsewhere or escape their poverty-stricken existence. Serfdom gradually declined in England and western Europe in the 1400s, 1500s, and 1600s. But it survived in Russia and eastern Europe well into the 1800s, when the Industrial Revolution was in full sway in Britain and the United States.

In some soon-to-industrialize regions, meanwhile, out-and-out slavery largely

Weavers at their machines in England during the Industrial Revolution. It is often referred to as the "machine age" because of the large number of machines that were invented.

Russian serfs at their plows. Serfdom continued in Russia many years after the Industrial Revolution began in Great Britain and the United States.

replaced serfdom. As Northeastern University scholar Laura L. Frader explains:

> In North America and the Caribbean, African and African-American slaves labored on plantations, working in cotton, tobacco, and sugar cane fields. . . . The [use of slaves] permitted many British, French, and Spanish merchants to make huge profits. Some of these profits were later invested in industry and slave-produced cotton became essential for the Industrial Revolution.[1]

Whether they were free, semifree, or unfree, those hundreds of millions who worked the land across Europe and the rest of world had certain things in common prior to the machine age. First, they used simple, nonmechanized equipment and traditional methods, including handheld tools such as hoes and sickles and animals such as donkeys or oxen to pull plows. They "relied on rudimentary equipment and time-honored practices," Frader points out.

Both men and women planted, cultivated, and harvested, while children and young people helped. Young people also milked cows, churned butter, gathered eggs, and fed farm animals. Similar activities occupied both men and women in early nineteenth-century rural families in [areas] of the world as far apart as Sweden, Japan, and some parts of eastern Europe. [Among freeborn farmers], many families produced surpluses of agricultural produce, small animals and poultry, cheese, butter, and eggs to sell locally in market towns. In many communities, neighbors shared, bartered, and donated their labor to help each other out.[2]

Cottage Industries

Food was not the only commodity produced by hand in preindustrial society. Manufacturing—of clothing, tools, weapons, tableware, and other essential goods—was also accomplished by hand using simple tools, most of which had been around since ancient times. These included rudimentary distaffs for spinning yarn and basic hand-driven looms to weave the yarn into cloth. Moreover, there was little or no division of labor. That is, one or two people completed most or all of the steps in making a product, or they did some of the steps and hired a neighbor to finish off the process. In contrast, the later machine age featured factories in which each worker specialized in a single, specialized task, constituting only a small step in the overall process.

This preindustrial manufacturing took place either in people's homes or in

A Family Enterprise

In preindustrial Europe, it was common for all members of a rural family to get involved in home-manufacturing processes, including making clothes. They often performed these duties while keeping up with planting, harvesting, threshing, and other farm-related tasks. Irish writer James Orr (1770–1816) captured some of this busy, diligent activity in his poem "The Penitent," excerpted here:

He [the father] weaved himself, and kept
  two or three [looms] going,

Who praised him for strong, well-handled
  yarn.

His thrifty wife and wise, wee [small] lasses [daughters] span [do the measuring].

While warps and quills [weaving components] employed another child,

Some [members of the family arose] each morn and threshed [the grain]. . . .

Some learned the question-book [schoolbook] in neighboring barn [in addition to their regular duties].

Quoted in Laura L. Frader and Sonya O. Rose, eds., *Gender and Class in Modern Europe.* Ithaca, NY: Cornell University Press, 1996, pp. 37–38.

small workshops owned by merchants. Over time, this approach became known as cottage industry. It was not only small in scale but also very slow, methodical, and often tedious for the workers.

Also, because cottage industries utilized simple tools wielded almost solely by hand, the volume of production was limited. In other words, a single family or a small group of craftsmen in a workshop could turn out only a small number of products in a given week, month, or year. That meant that a limited quantity of everyday goods was available to the

A woman reenacts the process of spinning wool by hand. Prior to the Industrial Revolution, people who made goods for sale did it by hand, usually in their own homes.

residents of a given region. Those who could make or afford to buy essential goods maintained at least minimal levels of comfort. Those who could neither make nor buy such basics lived in poverty far more desperate and squalid than the worst endured in modern industrialized societies.

Yet despite the drawbacks of preindustrial agriculture and manufacturing, these institutions instilled in the workers (at least the freeborn ones) feelings of accomplishment, independence, and self-sufficiency. A nineteenth-century English physician named Peter Gaskell, who felt that many aspects of life had been better before the Industrial Revolution, explained it this way:

> By all the processes being carried on under a man's own roof, he retained his individual respectability. He was kept apart from associations that might injure his moral worth, and he generally earned wages which were . . . sufficient to live comfortably on. . . . The domestic manufacturers were scattered over the entire surface of the country. Themselves cultivators, and of simple habits and few wants, they rarely left their own homesteads.[3]

Substandard Living Conditions

Another reason why most people seldom strayed far from their homes or immediate neighborhoods was due to the primitive state of transportation in preindustrial society. Cars, trains, airplanes, steamboats, and other advanced forms of transport—all inventions and hallmarks of the machine age—did not yet exist. So people had to walk, ride horses, or ride in animal-drawn wagons or old-fashioned sailing ships.

By land, it took many days, or in some cases a couple of weeks, for the average person to travel only a few hundred miles. Boat trips were faster. But these were available mainly to those who lived in coastal regions, and passage was usually expensive. Thus, outside of some traders, government messengers, and religious pilgrims, few people felt that the effort to travel long distances was worth it.

Moreover, for centuries it was the few hardy individuals who did take long trips who carried news from one region to another. This was because people in preindustrial societies had something else in common—extremely basic means of communications. There was no telegraph, radio, television, or other electronic communications devices because these, too, were products of the industrial age and the technological revolutions that grew out of it.

Before the introduction of the electronic telegraph in the early 1800s, information moved by the same traditional and slow means that people did. (One exception was setting up signal fires or smoke signals on hilltops. Each was visible from a more distant hill in the line of sight, and a signal could be sent hundreds

Travelers at an inn in the 1700s. The difficulties of travel during this time period kept most people close to home.

of miles in less than a day. However, the system was not very practical. It required a lot of manpower and organization, and only the simplest of messages could be sent.)

Preindustrial life was also hampered by what today would be viewed as substandard housing and health conditions. As in all ages, a small number of wealthy people dwelled in luxury and comfort. But the bulk of the population—in both cities and the countryside—lived in cottages, houses, or apartments of extremely modest means. The typical home had a few small rooms. There was no central heating, no electricity, and very few houses had any sort of plumbing facili-

ties, including flush toilets. As a result, most people relied on fireplaces, warm clothing, and extra blankets for warmth; candles and oil lamps for light; streams or public fountains for drinking water; and outhouses to relieve themselves. (In towns and cities, some people used bedpans or buckets and periodically emptied them into alleyways, vacant lots, or streams.)

The lack of proper toilets, plumbing, sewers, and pure water sources did more than make various aspects of life inconvenient and uncomfortable. These and other factors also contributed to the primitive state of medicine and health in preindustrial times. The connection between germs and disease had not yet been discovered. (Like so many other scientific advances, that discovery would occur at the height of the Industrial Revolution.)

Out of ignorance, people of all walks of life regularly engaged in unsanitary practices. For these reasons, disease epidemics that killed tens of thousands or more were common occurrences in Europe and elsewhere. Moreover, the overall poor health conditions and low standard of living made life expectancy much lower than in postindustrial times. Average life expectancy in preindustrial Britain was between thirty and forty years. Today it is close to eighty.

A Great Historical Watershed

In many ways, therefore, everyday life was very different before the Industrial Revolution than it was after that great historical watershed. True, such factors as the rapid growth of cities and slums surrounding the factories produced poverty and substandard living conditions in the early years of industrialization. But as time went on, improvements in sanitation and medicine and the introduction of plumbing, electricity, and other advancements largely overcame these drawbacks. The general standard of living also rose thanks to increased overall economic prosperity in industrialized countries. As one expert observer puts it:

Perhaps the greatest benefits of industrialization are increased material well-being and improved healthcare for many people in industrial societies. Modern industrial life also provides a constantly changing flood of new goods and services, giving consumers more choices. [Because of these and other factors] the Industrial Revolution has been one of the most influential and far-reaching movements in human history.[4]

Chapter One

LIFE IN THE INDUSTRIAL TOWNS

The history of the lives of the workers of the Industrial Revolution is largely an urban—or town- and city-centered—one. This is because the rise of large-scale industry in Britain, the United States, and other countries also brought about a genuine urban revolution. First, a majority of factories and manufacturing workshops (in essence small factories) were located in urban areas. (By the late 1800s, more than 90 percent of American factories were in cities.) This was partly because cities were also hubs of transportation and shipping. And having their production facilities within or near these hubs made it easier and cheaper for big manufacturers to sell their goods to distant markets.

A second important factor in the urbanization of industry was that the manufacturers, often called industrialists, needed many people to work in their factories. At first, they found many of their recruits in rural areas. Agriculture had long been the predominant economic sector of society. But as the Industrial Revolution progressed and manufacturing came to dominate the economy, farming declined, leaving many residents of the countryside out of work. Often desperate, large numbers of them migrated to the cities to take the new factory jobs.

As a result, industrial towns in Britain, France, the United States, and other industrializing nations grew extremely rapidly in the nineteenth century and beyond. One of Britain's chief industrial centers, Manchester, had a mere 25,000 residents in 1770. By 1852 the city's population had increased by a whopping 1,400 percent, to 350,000 people, most of them factory workers and their families. And on the whole, Britain's population rose from 5.7 million in 1750 to 16.6 million in 1850. The United States experienced similar population increases as it industrialized. In 1860 only three American cities had 250,000 or more residents. By 1900, however, fourteen industrial cities met that condition; the biggest, New York City, boasted a population of about 1.5 million by 1890.

The many industrial workers who poured into the cities in the machine age swiftly separated into two distinct economic and social groups or classes. One was at first a relatively small middle class composed of small businessmen, factory managers and foremen, merchants, and others who made decent—and in some cases substantial—salaries. The second and much larger group was made up of the menial laborers. Frequently referred to as "the working class" or "ordinary workers," they typically earned very low wages, making it difficult for them to make ends meet. The differences between the living conditions of these proverbial haves and have-nots were stark to say the least.

Middle-Class Comforts

Most members of the middle class who were involved in some aspect of industry or the commerce it stimulated enjoyed comfortable lifestyles. They were far from rich, as were the handful of industrialists for whom they worked. But a factory manager or a merchant whose store sold the goods the factory

Manchester, England, was an industrial town that saw rapid population growth in the nineteenth century because of the availability of factory jobs.

Industrial work allowed many members of the middle class to live a comfortable lifestyle. However, the life of a domestic servant was one of drudgery and low pay.

produced could afford to own or rent a single-family home. Frequently it was a modest two- or three-story townhouse in a well-kept, relatively safe section of town. More often than not, such families could afford to send their children to good schools. And some could afford to hire a maid or other servant (commonly called a "domestic") to help with housekeeping duties.

With rare exceptions, the wife (or mother or other leading family female) ran the household while her husband was off at work. Some idea of her varied duties and the setting in which she lived comes from an 1861 book. Written by an Englishwoman named Isabella Beeton, it gave advice to middle-class women on how best to manage their homes. "As with the commander of an army," Beeton writes,

so it is with the mistress of a house. Her spirit will be seen through the whole establishment [and] her domestics [will] follow in her path. . . . Frugality and economy are home virtues, without which no household can prosper. . . . A housekeeping account book should invariably be kept, and kept punctually and precisely. [Such] accounts should be balanced not less than once a month. [Also] once a month it is advisable that the mistress [examine] her store of glass and china [tableware], marking any breakages on the inventory of these articles. . . . The treatment of servants is of the highest [importance]. If they perceive that the mistress's conduct is regulated by high and correct principles, they will not fail to respect her. [In the spring] winter curtains should be taken down and replaced by the summer white ones; and furs and woolen clothes also carefully [packed away].[5]

A Busy Middle-Class Woman

During the Industrial Revolution, many middle-class women found themselves busy night and day with household duties, social causes, and other activities. Writer Lydia Maria Child documented her own activities for the year 1864 in her diary. These examples represent only a small portion of the total list.

Wrote 235 letters, wrote six articles for newspapers . . . wrote my will . . . read aloud [to a public audience] six pamphlets and 21 volumes, read to myself 7 volumes . . . knit two pairs of hospital socks [and] six baby shirts for friends, knit one large Afghan and made the fringe . . . made 1 lined woolen cape . . . cut and made three gowns . . . made 4 pillow cases . . . mended 70 pairs of stockings, cooked 360 dinners, cooked 362 breakfasts, swept and dusted sitting-room and kitchen 350 times . . . made 5 visits to aged women . . . made 7 calls upon neighbors.

Quoted in Gerda Lerner, *The Female Experience: An American Documentary*. Indianapolis: Bobbs-Merrill, 1979, pp. 125–26.

People who read Beeton's book and could afford to own both winter and summer curtains usually held themselves aloof from ordinary workers. There was little social contact between the two classes, in the sense of strong friendships, dinner parties, and shared leisure time. This was because most members of the middle class did not view working-class people as their social equals.

The two groups did intermingle regularly, however, in two settings. One was at work, where a factory or store manager oversaw a number of laborers or clerks, whom he could order around or fire at will. The other intersection of the two classes was the relationship between master and servant alluded to by Beeton. These servants, usually women, almost always received little pay. For most of them, their employment was a form of exploitation that brought them little in return but that greatly benefited their bosses. As Frader points out:

> The working-class women who took these [servant] jobs participated in the private and intimate lives of their employers on a daily basis, helping them dress, cleaning their clothes, caring for their children, and nursing them when sick. Indeed, the labor of working-class women and men enabled middle-class men and women to enjoy lives of relative leisure and to engage in reform activities or intellectual pur-

suits. The middle-class clearly prospered. The working-class standard of living was another matter.[6]

Tenements and Slums

Indeed, the workers' living sphere, though located in the same city, was in many ways a world apart from that of the middle class. Of the many downsides of life for workers in the nineteenth-century industrial towns, overcrowding was the most obvious, basic, and problematic. Because of the sheer numbers of people who moved to the cities, builders could not keep up with the incessant demand for more housing. Thus, they threw up new dwellings as fast as they could, with only minimal concern for quality and durability.

Also, the vast majority of these new residents were low paid and poor. They could not afford to buy or rent comfortable accommodations, as members of the middle class could. As a result, much of the workers' housing erected in this era consisted of tenements. These were large, multistoried structures, each containing many small, inexpensive apartments. Often clustered around the factories, they swiftly grew into sprawling slums.

A number of contemporary written descriptions and photographs of these run-down neighborhoods have survived. Among the more vivid are those of Jacob Riis (1849–1914), a Danish American journalist and photographer. He documented the harsh lives of poor

Several workers share a cramped room in New York City in 1890. Overcrowding and low pay were two of the downsides for workers who lived in industrial cities.

industrial workers and tenement dwellers in New York City in the late 1800s. Riis described a typical tenement apartment as a set of rooms consisting of a couple of closet-sized bedrooms and a living room measuring 10 by 12 feet (3 by 4m). The latter, in which most family activities took place, was about the size of a small bedroom in an average modern American house. Few tenement buildings had indoor plumbing or toilets, Riis pointed out. In many cases, one or two sinks and toilets were located in an adjacent yard, and the dozens or hundreds of people who lived in the building shared them. Furniture was also scarce

New York's Crowded Tenements

Danish American journalist and photographer Jacob Riis toured and wrote about the tenements and other aspects of the lives of industrial workers in nineteenth-century New York City. In this excerpt from his widely read book, How the Other Half Lives, *he discusses the problem of overcrowding.*

The tenement-house population had swelled to half a million souls [and] on the East Side, in what is still the most densely populated district in all the world

. . . it was packed at the rate of 290,000 to the square mile. [In comparison] the greatest crowding of Old London was at the rate of 175,816. Swine roamed the streets and gutters [of the New York tenements] as their principal scavengers. The death of a child in a tenement was registered at the Bureau of Vital Statistics as "plainly due to suffocation in the foul air of an unventilated apartment."

Jacob A. Riis, *How the Other Half Lives: Studies Among the Tenements of New York.* New York: Scribner's, 1907, p. 10.

in these structures. A government study conducted of New York City tenements during that era found that it was common for three, four, or more persons to share the same bed.

According to Riis and other observers, the tenements alone did not meet the ever-growing demand for cheap urban housing. Therefore, many existing single-family homes were purchased by factory owners, builders, landlords, or others. They subdivided each of these dwellings into several tiny apartments. In Riis's words:

[As] the city grew with rapid strides, the necessities of the poor became the opportunity of their wealthier neighbors, and the stamp was set upon the old houses, suddenly become valuable. . . . Their *"large rooms were partitioned into several smaller ones,* without regard to light or ventilation [according to a government report quoted by Riis], the rate of rent being lower in proportion to space or height from the street; and they soon became filled from cellar to garret [loft] with [people]." Worse was to follow. It was "soon perceived by estate owners and agents of property that a greater percentage of profits could be realized by the conversion of houses and blocks into barracks, and dividing their space into smaller proportions capable of containing human life within four walls."[7]

Sometimes the overcrowding of both the tenements and subdivided houses was made even worse by the financial desperation of the tenants. Trying to make an extra buck, some families took on their own boarders, some of whom slept in closets or attic crawl spaces.

Living in Slums

Considering the extent of overcrowding, the residents' poverty, and landlords' greed, repairs and even regular upkeep were rare in the industrial slums. So urban blight and filthy, unsavory living conditions became common in them. A French physician named Alphonse Guépin was appalled by what he observed in 1835 in a workers' slum in France's rapidly growing industrial town of Nantes:

If you want to know how [the worker] lives, go [to Nantes's industrial slum]. Pass through one of those drain-like openings below street level, that lead to those filthy

A boy overlooks a slum outside of Paris in the mid-nineteenth century. Filthy, polluted, and disgusting have all been used to describe the slums in nineteenth-century European industrial towns.

dwellings, but remember to stoop as you enter. One must have gone down into these alleys where the atmosphere is as damp and cold as a cellar. One must have known what it is like to feel one's foot slip on the polluted ground and to fear a stumble into the filth [and] to realize the painful impression that one receives on entering the homes of these unfortunate workers. Below street-level on each side of the passage there is a large, gloomy, cold room. Foul water oozes out of the walls. Air reaches the room through a sort of semi-circular window. . . . Go in, if the fetid [rotten] smell that assails you does not make you recoil.[8]

The situation Guépin describes was unfortunately the rule rather than the exception in nineteenth-century European industrial towns. In 1845 German writer Friedrich Engels observed strikingly similar living conditions in a workers' slum in the large English industrial town of Manchester. He described "a filth and disgusting grime, the equal of which is not to be found." He also recalled "the most horrible dwellings which I have yet beheld" and went on to say:

In one of these courts there stands directly at the entrance, at the end of the covered passage, a privy [toilet stall] without a door, so dirty that the inhabitants can pass into and out of the court only by pass-

ing through foul pools of stagnant urine and excrement. . . . Here, as in most of the working-men's quarters of Manchester, the pork-raisers rent the courts and build pig-pens in them. In almost every court one or even several such pens may be found, into which the inhabitants of the court throw all refuse and offal [guts of butchered animals], whence the swine grow fat; and the atmosphere, confined on all four sides, is utterly corrupted by putrefying [rotting] animal and vegetable substances.[9]

Some towns did have sewers. This helped the tenement dwellers because they could throw their refuse and human and animal wastes into them. However, many industrial cities lacked sewers until the middle or even late 1800s. As late as the 1850s, for example, London, one of the world's biggest urban centers, had yet to install sewers. Thus, people dumped their wastes into thousands of shallow underground pits, which laborers known as nightsoil men emptied on an irregular basis. Over time, large numbers of these cesspools were neglected. Eventually, they overflowed and their repulsive contents seeped through floorboards and wall cracks in houses and tenement buildings.

A High Risk of Disease

It is hardly surprising that such unsanitary conditions were as unhealthy as

This political cartoon from 1852 blames the unsanitary conditions in London's slums for the spread of cholera.

they were unsightly and smelly. Part of the problem was the widespread filth and contamination itself. But an equally important factor was ignorance about the causes of disease. Up until the mid-1800s, no one realized that germs cause a long list of diseases and that the unsanitary conditions were breeding grounds for germs. Likewise, poor hygiene practices stemming from that ignorance regularly contributed to epidemics both small and large.

Among the most frequent and most feared diseases to strike the industrial towns during this period was cholera. Caused by drinking water contaminated with a bacterium (a kind of germ) called *Vibrio cholerae,* its symptoms include severe diarrhea, dehydration, and nausea. Untreated victims often die. Cholera epidemics struck British cities, especially their industrial slums, in 1831–1832, 1848–1849, 1854, and 1867. Some fifteen thousand people died in the 1848–1849 outbreak. As many as thirty thousand perished in 1854.

Other diseases ravaged the industrial towns before the late 1800s and early 1900s, when scientific strides and improvements in sanitation significantly reduced the risk of contagion. Typhoid fever, another ailment caused by germ-contaminated water, was prominent among them. But the most devastating killer was tuberculosis (TB). "The disease caused a wasting of the body with the lungs being attacked," according to one modern expert.

> TB affected those who had been poorly fed and were under-nourished. It also affected those who lived in dirty and damp homes. TB can be spread by a person breathing in the exhaled sputum [coughed-up materials] of someone who already has the disease. In the overcrowded tenements of the industrial cities, one infected person could spread the disease very easily. Though accurate records are difficult to acquire, it is believed that TB killed one-third of all those who died in Britain between 1800 and 1850.[10]

Struggles at Home

The discomforts of overcrowding and the dangers of disease were not the only factors that affected the home lives of lower-class industrial workers. They also struggled to maintain traditional family structure, unity, and gender roles. First, the vast majority of working-class families could not survive on the income of a single worker, which tradition designated to be the husband-father. In many cases, the wife-mother also had to work. And so did some or all of the children.

In fact, working-class families had to learn to adapt to a wide range of household scenarios, none of which were seen as ideal. When both parents worked outside the home, for example, the older children (or, when possible, grandparents or other relatives) had to look after infants and toddlers and maintain the house. This was a major commitment because factory shifts often lasted fourteen or more hours per day, six or even seven days per week.

A different set of dynamics and problems ensued if the mother worked outside the home and the father did not. (He might be disabled in some way or temporarily unable to find work. Or the local factories might prefer hiring women.) This happened fairly often in the early decades of the Industrial Revolution, when large numbers of women worked in textile mills in Britain and the United States. Many people viewed this nontraditional family situation as topsy-turvy, even unnatural. In his study of industrial conditions in Manchester, England, in the 1840s, Engels observed that hundreds of stay-at-home men were "condemned to domestic occupations" in a home life "turned upside down." With an attitude that today would be considered narrow and sexist, he added:

It is easy to imagine the wrath aroused among the workingmen by this reversal of all relations within the family while the other social conditions remain unchanged. Can anyone imagine a more insane state of things? . . . Yet this condition, which unsexes the man and takes from the woman all womanliness [and] degrades in the most shameful way both sexes [is] the final [and pathetic] achievement of all the efforts and struggles of hundreds of generations to improve [humanity's lot].[11]

During the second half of the Industrial Revolution, fewer women worked outside the home, and the traditional concept of the male breadwinner once more became firmly entrenched. However, this also changed family dynamics. With the husband gone more than fourteen hours a day, a wife had to assume almost all household duties. As was also true in middle-class families,

To make ends meet, entire families would often engage in additional work at home.

this included taking charge of the family finances. It became common for the husband to turn over all of his weekly earnings to his wife. She then gave him a small portion of the total as an allowance and used the rest, according to her personal judgment, to keep the household running. In the 1870s a British writer who called herself Lady Bell described a working-class family in which the working husband made twenty-five shillings (then roughly equivalent to six American dollars) per week:

> She gives him 2 [shillings] a week for pocket money. [In many such families] the woman has the upper hand, in spite of the wages being earned by the husband and her receiving them from him, she makes a favor of the amount she gives him back again.[12]

Still another nontraditional household dynamic was created when most or all of the family members made money at home. Some industrial laborers turned their homes into workplaces where they could manufacture certain products to supplement the family income. "For many working-class families," Frader writes,

> the boundaries between public work and private domestic life continually blurred. Although the Industrial Revolution transformed numerous jobs, workers continued to manufacture some goods, such as clothing, at home since they required no special equipment beyond a needle and thread or a sewing machine.[13]

In such situations, it was common for the father, mother, and all but the youngest children to huddle around the kitchen table, which doubled as a work table. Employing division of labor techniques borrowed from the factories, each person would do a specific step in the process over and over again. This would go on for twelve or more hours each day, for at least six days a week.

Unable to Escape

Indeed, whether they toiled in factories or in their own homes, the poorer workers put in extremely long hours by today's standards. And the financial rewards were usually pitifully small. Combined with the squalor and diseases rampant in the slums, one result was that many workers felt locked into a grim, unhappy situation they could neither control nor escape. It is not surprising, then, that mental depression and alcoholism were common illnesses that plagued life in the industrial slums. According to a modern expert on alcoholism:

> In the easy-going household workshops and cottage manufacturing of pre-industrial England, drinking meant friendship and sociability. With the advent of the Industrial Revolution, however, a new class of working people was created,

[and] their heavy drinking was, to a large extent, associated with their subordinate and exploited status. . . . Alcohol abuse occurred in England during the Industrial Revolution when workers [lived in horrendous filth and] poverty. Under these conditions alcohol was consumed to obtain relief from stress and oblivion from misery.[14]

Thus, urban poverty and blight, cramped living conditions, disease epidemics, altered family structure and roles, and substance abuse all helped to shape life in the growing industrial cities. It was not until the twentieth century that these ills became far less common. A number of factors contributed. But the main remedy proved to be rising prosperity, itself another important outcome of the Industrial Revolution. Over time, more and more members of the working class were able to enter the middle class, which became the most powerful social force in modern societies.

Chapter Two

CONDITIONS IN INDUSTRIAL WORKPLACES

Whatever conditions and problems the workers of the Industrial Revolution endured at home, together these constituted only one of the two major aspects of their lives. The other consisted of the time they were working and the conditions they encountered in factories, mines, and other workplaces. In fact, most industrial workers spent more time at work than they did at home. And the conditions that prevailed at work affected them in numerous ways, both physically and mentally.

For the most part, middle-class workers, such as factory managers and merchants, benefited from the industrial system. They made comfortable, or at least adequate, salaries. And their working conditions were usually acceptable. This was partly because they were often in supervisory positions and usually did not have to handle potentially dangerous machines or tools or to perform repetitive acts day in and day out. Also, they could afford to take time off periodically for relaxation and leisure pursuits; most ordinary workers did not have this luxury. Therefore, modern examinations of working conditions in British and U.S. industry in the nineteenth and early twentieth centuries concentrate mainly on the experiences, complaints, and overall plight of working-class laborers.

Long Hours, Low Wages

The first complaint that a majority of industrial workers had was that their workdays were too long. The average number of hours in a shift varied from industry to industry, from place to place, and from era to era. Workers in British and American textile mills in the early to middle 1800s generally put in twelve- to fifteen-hour days, for instance. They usually worked six days a week, with only Sundays off. Their average workweek was seventy-eight hours.

In contrast were the hours of workers who labored in American steel mills in the late 1800s. The length of their shifts was determined by the fact that the blast furnaces they tended almost always operated twenty-four hours a day. (In large part, this was because it was too time-consuming and costly to shut down a furnace at night and reheat it to the desired temperature the next morning.) Thus, it became customary for steel mills to have two twelve-hour shifts. However, many of the steel workers labored seven days a week. That gave them a workweek of eighty-four hours. Moreover, sometimes they had to put in extra hours on top of this demanding schedule. Not long after 1900, Charles M. Cabot, a Boston man who owned stock in the U.S. Steel Company, toured several steel mills. He was appalled by

A political cartoon from 1883 shows the effects of high rents and low wages on a poor family as an unfeeling landlord comes to collect his money.

the length of the workers' shifts and reported in a newspaper article:

A twelve-hour man, you would naturally think, would be relieved by a man on the shift at the end of his twelve hours. He generally is. But I have talked . . . with twelve-hour steel workers who have been obliged to work thirty-six hours at a stretch because the other man did not relieve them.[15]

Despite the minor differences in the length of workweeks from one industry to another, the average worker put in twelve- to fourteen-hour days at least six days a week. This grueling schedule remained more or less standard well into the twentieth century. It was not until 1920 that a fifty-hour workweek was introduced in the United States. And a forty-hour week did not become the rule in most industries until 1938.

Low wages was another common complaint of industrial workers. For example, early textile workers in both Britain and America made extremely little money. In part this was because many of them were women, who traditionally made less than men for doing the same job. In 1845 a New York newspaper reported:

A great number of females are employed in making men's and boys' caps. By constant labor . . . they can make 14 to 25 cents [per day]. We are told by an old lady

who has lived by this kind of work for a long time that when she begins at sunrise and works till midnight, she can earn [only] 14 cents a day.[16]

A few years later, in 1851, the average wage earned by American industrial workers in general was seven to ten dollars per week. That same year New York's *Daily Tribune* reported that a worker's family of five required just over ten dollars a week just for basics such as rent, food, and fuel. "Where is the money to pay for amusements," the editor asked, "to pay for doctor or apothecary [medicine], to pay for pew rent in the church, to purchase books, musical instruments?"[17] The obvious answer was that most ordinary workers could not afford many simple comforts that middle-class workers enjoyed. This unfortunate situation endured in America for decades to come and improved only slowly. As late as 1912, a study found that only 15 percent of working-class families made wages above subsistence level (the bare minimum needed to survive), 45 percent were at that level, and 40 percent were below it.

Discomforts and Drawbacks

Early industrial workers had many other workplace issues to deal with besides long hours and low wages. They received no sick pay or old-age pensions, for instance. Such benefits did not become common in British and American indus-

Garment workers sew in a crowded sweatshop in the 1890s. The nature of industrial work meant that workers performed a single task over and over.

try until well into the twentieth century. Moreover, most factories and businesses actually withheld some of a worker's wages if he or she was too sick to go to work.

In addition, the nature of most industrial work, along with the atmosphere within factories, took a toll on the workers both physically and psychologically. First, division of labor, in which each worker accomplished a single step in the manufacturing process, became widespread in industry. It forced the average laborer to perform the same task over and over again, day after day, month after month, and year after year. Writing in 1904, an expert observer pointed out:

> The benumbing [deadening] power of factory labor lies not so much in its hardness as its monotony. [Doing] the same small task over and over again [causes mental] dullness, apathy, [and] a mechanical and stolid [indifferent] spirit without vivacity [energy] or hope.[18]

This repetitiveness and monotony had a particularly harmful effect on workers who had moved to cities from agricultural areas. On their farms they had been used to performing a number of diverse tasks in a typical workday.

Some workers tried to relieve the boredom by striking up conversations with fellow workers or, when they could get away with it, sneaking away to go for a walk or take a nap. This reduced a factory's efficiency and output, of course. Therefore, many employers set strict rules, such as forbidding talking among the workers. A few owners even locked the doors or surrounded their factories

The Coming of Scientific Management

The following concise description of scientific management, a tool used by various industries to improve efficiency and output, is by Northeastern University scholar Edward G. Wertheim.

The Industrial Revolution [and] creation of large factories in the late Eighteenth Century . . . created tremendous challenges to organization and management that had not been confronted before. [The] most important of those who began to create a science of management was Frederic Winslow Taylor (1856–1915). . . . His model was the machine with its cheap, interchangeable parts, each of which does one specific function. . . . Just as machine parts were easily interchangeable, cheap, and passive [Taylor said], so too should the human parts be the same. [The] overall goal was to remove human variability. The results were profound. Productivity under Taylorism went up dramatically. . . . Rational rules replaced trial and error; management became formalized and efficiency increased. Of course, this did not come about without resistance. . . . Many workers resisted what some considered the "dehumanization of work" [and] the industrial engineer with his stop watch and clip-board, standing over you measuring . . . one's [smallest] movements became a hated figure and led to much sabotage and group resistance.

Edward G. Wertheim, "Historical Background of Organizational Behavior." http://web.cba.neu.edu/~ewertheim/introd/history.htm.

with walls to keep workers from leaving the grounds during their shift. By the early 1900s, a number of employers resorted to hiring efficiency experts who advocated "scientific management." In essence, it imposed rules and practices that eliminated time and waste in each manufacturing step; but this only increased workers' boredom and made them feel even more like cogs in a giant machine.

In addition to such psychological strain, many industrial workers endured physical strains and discomforts. Many factories had little ventilation, for example. This made the air stale, heavy, and hard to breathe. Excessive heat was another common problem, especially in iron foundries, steel mills, and cotton mills. In the latter, the owners purposely kept the temperature high because cotton threads break less often when the air is hot and humid. William Cobbett, a British journalist who visited several cotton mills in Britain during the 1820s, reported that interior temperatures commonly reached 84 degrees Fahrenheit (29°C). The workers, he said, had

> not a moment to wipe off the sweat, and not a breath of [fresh] air [for hours at a time]. The door of the [mill] is *locked,* except *half an hour* [a day, and] the workpeople are not allowed to send for water to drink. . . . In addition to the heat . . . [there is] the *dust,* and what is called the *cotton-flyings,* or fuzz, which the unfortunate [workers] have to inhale.[19]

Exposed to such conditions on a regular basis, Cobbett wrote, many workers suffered from poor health and/or seemed to grow old before their time. Cobbett's countryman, physician Peter Gaskell, who also visited a number of cotton mills, confirmed the physical deterioration of many workers. "An uglier set of men and women, of boys and girls," he said, "it would be impossible to congregate in a smaller" confined area.

> Their complexion is sallow [pale] and pallid [pasty]—with a peculiar flatness of feature [sunken cheeks]. Their stature [is] low, the average height of four hundred men, measured at different times, and different places, being five feet six inches. Their limbs [are] slender and [many have] a very general bowing of the legs. Great numbers of girls and women walk lamely or awkwardly, with raised chests and spinal flexures. Nearly all have flat feet.[20]

Workplace Dangers

In a number of factories and mines, working conditions not only adversely affected workers' long-term health but also posed more immediate dangers. It was not uncommon, for example, for workers to get fingers, arms, or legs caught in machines. Men and boys who worked in coal mines sometimes got their hands caught in conveyers (machines that carried coal from one place to another). And in textile mills,

Miners were especially vulnerable to deadly industrial accidents, including explosions of dangerous gases in the mines.

some women and children got their hair caught in power looms and other machines. On occasion, a worker dozed off for a few seconds, lost his or her balance, and fell into a large machine. The result was permanent disfigurement or death. Burns were also common injuries in industrial facilities, especially in steel mills and other places where people worked alongside fires or furnaces.

Making matters worse, in most cases there were few or no safety features or procedures on site. Most employers felt that spending money on such things cut too much into their profits. Furthermore, they usually accepted no responsibility for accidents when they occurred and offered no financial compensation to injured workers. For a long time, there was a common-law doctrine, or unwritten rule, that a worker who took an industrial job accepted any and all risks of injury on that job. With the exception of U.S. Steel (beginning in 1901) and a handful of others, American companies did not offer disability or death benefits before the 1920s.

As a result, throughout the late 1700s, 1800s, and early 1900s, large numbers of industrial workers were injured or killed on the job. Each year between 1880 and 1900, about 350,000 Americans suffered workplace injuries. And roughly 35,000 were killed in factories, mines, and other industrial workplaces.

Coal mining proved particularly dangerous. That industry alone produced some two thousand worker deaths per year in the last decades of the nineteenth century. One danger was flooding of mine shafts by underground streams and water tables. Mines were equipped with pumps to keep water levels low; but sometimes the pumps broke down or were unable to cope with a sudden, massive influx of water.

Other dangers included inhaling coal dust (which causes black lung disease) and poor ventilation. The air in deep galleries (the tunnels where the miners worked) quickly became stale and unhealthy. To provide fresh air to the miners it was routine to install a furnace or fire at the bottom of one or more vertical mine shafts. Rising heat from this source drew air from the galleries upward, partially ventilating them. However, methane gas, a common byproduct of coal mining, was present in varying quantities in the circulating air. Because it is highly flammable (prone to catching fire), the methane sometimes reacted with the flames, causing explosions or fires.

Industrial Disasters

Fire from the ventilating furnace might also ignite some of the timbers lining the shafts and galleries. This is what happened in the infamous Avondale disaster, one of the worst industrial accidents in U.S. history. On September 6, 1869, sparks from a ventilating furnace at the Avondale mine near Plymouth, Pennsylvania, started a fire that spread quickly through the mine. The flames destroyed the only exit the miners had for escape.

Firemen douse the upper floors of the Triangle Shirtwaist Company in New York City after a fire caused the deaths of 146 workers. After this tragedy, safety rules began to be passed to protect workers.

The fire also swiftly used up the oxygen in the galleries. Noted nineteenth-century coal miner, mine inspector, and author Andrew Roy penned a lengthy description of the catastrophe, saying in part:

> A cloud of smoke, followed by a mass of living flame, rose through the upcast compartment of the mine. . . . The people on top of the shaft became paralyzed with terror, knowing the fate of the miners in the distant chambers of the mine. . . . The news of the accident spread like wild-fire, and people rushed to the burning mine in thousands, to assist in rescuing the imperiled miners; but they were powerless before the burning elements. . . . The ponderous pulley wheels, ropes, and all the incombustible material above the pit's mouth, fell crashing through the shaft, followed by pieces of burning timbers and other debris. On the arrival of the fire engines, streams of water were turned into the burning mine; but the monster volume of lurid flame appeared to bid defiance to the water, and for several hours the fire raged with unabated fury.[21]

The final death toll was 110, including 5 teenaged boys and 2 of the rescuers.

In response to the Avondale calamity, Pennsylvania created new safety rules for its coal-mining industry. Similarly, other industrial disasters brought the dangers many workers faced to the attention of the public and lawmakers. One of the most notorious was the Triangle Shirtwaist factory fire, the worst industrial catastrophe in New York City's history. More than five hundred employees, most of them women, worked in the company's ten-story building near Washington Square. They made women's blouses, at the time commonly called shirtwaists, or more simply "waists."

The trouble began in the afternoon of March 25, 1911, when a fire began on the eighth floor. (The cause remains uncertain; one often-cited possibility is faulty electrical wiring.) The workers on most floors were fortunately alerted in time to escape. But by the time the women on the ninth floor learned what was happening, it was too late. Of their two escape routes, one had been locked by the owners and the other, a stairwell, was already engulfed in flames and smoke. Many of the terrified women jumped out of windows and plunged nine stories to their deaths. One of the many eyewit-nesses on the street, William G. Shepherd, later penned a graphic, agonizing account that stated in part:

I learned a new sound—a more horrible sound than description can picture. It was the thud of a speeding, living body on a stone sidewalk. I looked up—saw that there were scores of girls at the windows. The flames from the floor below were beating in their faces. Somehow I knew that they, too, must come down. . . . I even watched one girl falling. Waving her arms, trying to keep her body upright until the very instant she struck the

A Disaster Remembered in Song

These are some of the lyrics to one of several popular songs written in the mid-1800s to commemorate the notorious Avondale mine disaster.

On the sixth day of September,
    Eighteen sixty-nine,
Those miners all then got a call
    To go work in the mine;
But little did they think that [day]
    That death would soon prevail
Before they would return again from
    The mines of Avondale.
The women and their children,
    Their hearts were filled with joy

To see their men go to their work
    Likewise every boy;
But a dismal sight in broad daylight,
    Soon made them turn pale,
When they saw the breaker burning
    O'er the mines of Avondale.
From here and there and everywhere
    They gathered in a crowd,
Some tearing off their clothes and hair,
    And crying out aloud;
"Get out our husbands and our sons
    Death he's going to steal
Their lives away without delay
    In the mines of Avondale."

Quoted in Mudcat Café, "The Avondale Mine Disaster." www.mudcat.org/@displaysong.cfm?SongID=5778.

sidewalk, she was trying to balance herself. Then came the thud—then a silent, unmoving pile of clothing and twisted, broken limbs. . . . What I had seen before was not so terrible as what had followed. Up in the [ninth] floor girls were burning to death before our very eyes. They were jammed in the windows. . . . One by one . . . down came the bodies in a shower of burning, smoking, flaming bodies.[22]

In all, including those who jumped and those overcome by smoke and flames, 146 workers died in the fire. The public was horrified. And lawmakers soon began passing safety rules for industrial workplaces.

Dehumanizing Sweatshops

The Triangle Shirtwaist factory fire also exposed another aspect of the plight of industrial workers of that era. Although the Triangle facility was a factory, it was an example of a specific kind of factory known as a sweatshop. Sweatshops are industrial workplaces that resemble the large communal workrooms of preindustrial times. The main difference is that sweatshops feature at least some machines and usually utilize division of labor and other classic industrial methods.

The majority of sweatshops in America during the Industrial Revolution made clothes. They employed from as few as three or four to as many as several hundred workers. And they varied in size from one or two small rooms to multistoried buildings like the one that housed the Triangle Shirtwaist Company. Sweatshops began to appear in U.S. urban industrial centers during the 1840s and 1850s and reached their peak between 1880 and 1920. Experts estimate that in 1910 New York City alone had upwards of thirty thousand garment sweatshops that together employed about half a million workers.

No matter what their size or how many workers they had, sweatshops almost always had certain things in common. Typically they were located in run-down tenements or old office buildings that had been converted into workhouses. Many of these places were poorly lit, so workers often had to strain their eyes. And those workrooms without windows were badly ventilated, which made the air stale and oppressive. In addition, an average sweatshop ranged from untidy to filthy and crawling with cockroaches. In his book about New York City industrial workers, Jacob Riis touches on some of these ills, which he observed in one of the many sweatshops he inspected:

Men and women bend over their machines, or iron clothes. . . . [A visitor walks] through an endless work-room where [hapless workers] are forever laboring. Morning, noon, or night . . . the scene is always the same. . . . Up two flights of dark stairs, [or] three, [or] four [flights, where] whirring sewing machines

A foreman berates a sweatshop worker at her sewing machine. Sweatshop workers often had to endure poor treatment by their managers and owners.

behind closed doors betray what goes on within. . . . Five men and a woman, two young girls, not fifteen, and a boy who says unasked that he is fifteen, and lies in saying it, are at the machines sewing [pants]. The floor is littered ankle-deep with half-sewn garments.

[The] faces, hands, and arms to the elbows of everyone in the room are black with the color of the cloth on which they are working.[23]

Poor treatment of the workers was another hallmark of sweatshops. The employees despaired over their long

The Death of "Susie L"

Some sweatshop workers became so worn out and sick from the poor working conditions that they eventually died. One such case was reported in 1868 by a concerned social worker who investigated a dressmaking sweatshop in New York City. He called the young woman who died "Susie L":

The room is crowded with girls and women, most of whom are pale [and] are being robbed of life slowly and surely. The rose which should bloom in their cheeks has vanished long ago. The sparkle has gone out of their eyes. They bend over their work with aching backs and throbbing brows; sharp pains dart through their eyeballs; they breathe an atmosphere of death. . . . Susie L was a beautiful girl of seventeen, the daughter of a farmer in western New York. . . . Three months had not passed before she found her strength unequal to the task. . . . Dark lines had come under her eyes; her complexion was losing its color. . . . In a word, the poison had entered her system, and was killing her by degrees. . . . One day she dropped from her chair heavily upon the floor [and died].

Quoted in Leon Stein, ed., *Out of the Sweatshop: The Struggle for Industrial Democracy.* New York: Quadrangle, 1977, pp. 12–13.

hours, low pay, and the monotony of their repetitive tasks. They also resented that many of the owners and managers of these establishments treated them with little or no respect and looked on them as little better than slaves or human machines. The testimony of a sweatshop worker, Sadie Frowne, printed in an article in a New York newspaper in September 1902, describes some of the adverse working conditions she endured:

I get up at half-past five o'clock every morning and make myself a cup of coffee on the oil stove. I eat a bit of bread and perhaps some fruit and then go to work. . . . At seven o'clock we all sit down to our machines and the boss brings to each one the pile of work that he or she is to finish during the day. . . . Sometimes the work is not all finished by six o'clock, and then the one who is behind must work overtime. The machines go like mad all day. . . . Sometimes in my haste I get my finger caught and the needle goes right through it. [All] the time we are working the boss walks around examining the finished garments and making us do them over again if they are not just right.[24]

Among the most dehumanizing kinds of workplaces during the Industrial Revolution, sweatshops declined rapidly after 1920. New laws that mandated safer workplaces and better treatment of workers transformed the industrial sector. In 1938 widely read *Life* magazine declared the "war" on America's sweatshops won. A few reappeared in the 1960s and 1970s, however, as some unscrupulous bosses took advantage of new waves of poor, desperate foreign immigrants. Since that time, authorities have cleaned up or closed down the sweatshops that can be found. But a few of these appalling throwbacks to the great age of industrialization and worker exploitation still linger on.

Chapter Three

WOMEN WHO WORKED IN INDUSTRY

Following long-standing traditions dating back to medieval and even ancient times, women worked in Britain, the United States, France, and many other countries during the eighteenth and nineteenth centuries. Many belonged to farm families and helped their fathers or husbands plant, harvest, and raise livestock. Others spun and wove yarn and made clothes in cottage industries. And still others worked as tavern waitresses, shop assistants, and chambermaids and other servants.

It was perhaps only natural, therefore, that when the Industrial Revolution gained momentum in the late 1700s and early 1800s, some women were drawn into its working ranks. The jobs they performed in factories and other industrial workplaces varied widely. At first, most worked in textile mills. By 1826,

90 percent of the twelve hundred workers in the mills in Lowell, Massachusetts, were women. By 1860, sixty-two thousand women worked in textile mills in the New England region.

Women also rolled cigars and made straw hats, umbrellas, artificial flowers, and shoes and boots. By 1837 factories in the state of Massachusetts alone employed 15,000 women shoemakers. Large numbers of women also ran printing presses and other large machines in the printing industry. In 1831 a survey of print shops in Boston found that 395 of the 1,082 employees were women. There were even some female coal miners, especially in Britain.

These examples were part of an overall trend. As the machine age progressed, the number of women industrial workers continued to grow, both in Britain and the United States. By 1850, for example,

24 percent of all American workers in the manufacturing sector were women, numbering more than 225,000 in all. In the half-century that followed, that figure multiplied. When journalist Jacob Riis examined the sweatshops of New York City in the early 1900s, he estimated that a hefty proportion of the half-million people who toiled in these horrible conditions were women.

Female workers in a nineteenth-century textile mill. Factory owners hired women because they could pay them lower wages.

Home or Factory?

This rise of female industrial labor in the nineteenth and early twentieth centuries was a major new societal development and did not occur without considerable controversy. The industrialists who employed large numbers of women were not motivated by a sense of social justice. In other words, they did not hire women because they felt that females should have equal opportunities with men. Rather, they hired women mainly for selfish financial reasons. Factory and sweatshop owners knew that they could pay women less than men for the same work, so they could make more money by hiring women for certain jobs. (In 1831, for instance, male printers in Boston and other cities made about $1.50 a day; female printers made only one-third that amount.)

In fact, most men during that era, even the managers and laborers who worked alongside women, felt that women did not belong in factories. Instead, they belonged at home. A speaker at an 1866 meeting of a labor group, the International Working Men's Association, summed up this traditional societal, and predominantly male, view, saying:

> Women's place is in the home, near her children. She should watch over them and instruct them in the first principles [of life]. From the physical, moral, and social point of view, women's [wage] labor must be vigorously condemned as the principal

Working Women a Menace?

One of many influential men who felt that women did not belong in industry was labor leader Edward O'Donnell, who stated in 1897:

The rapid displacement of men by women in the factory and workshop has to be met sooner or later. . . . Is not this evolutionary backslide . . . a menace to prosperity—a foe to our civilized pretensions [aspirations]? The growing demand for female labor is not founded upon philanthropy [charity]. It does not spring from the milk of human kindness. It is an insidious [dangerous] assault upon the home. It is the knife of the assassin, aimed at the family circle. . . . The wholesale employment of women in the various [industries] must gradually unsex them [make them less feminine], as it most assuredly is demoralizing them [making them depressed] or stripping them of the modest demeanor that lends a charm to their kind.

Edward O'Donnell, "Women as Breadwinners: The Error of the Age," *American Federationist*, October 1897, p. 8.

[cause] of the degradation [ruin] of the race and as one of the capitalist [upper, industrialist] class's agents of demoralization [undermining the workers]. Nature has endowed women with predetermined functions. Her place is in the family! . . . The woman is the tie and the attraction that keeps the man at home, gives him habits of order and morality. . . . This is women's real work. It is a terrible mistake to impose another on her.[25]

A few men defended women's roles in industry, advocating that women had as much right to make a living that way as men did. Among these more progressive men, a handful even called for paying women the same wages as men for the same jobs. In 1868 a French labor activist named Paule Minck declared: "Equal pay for equal work! This is the only true justice. . . . It is about time that the scandalous [situation] of wage difference [between men and women] disappears forever."[26] Unfortunately for women workers, at the time such ideas were deemed highly radical. And it was not until the second half of the twentieth century that the movement toward equal pay for equal work began to make significant headway in industrialized countries.

Why Women Worked in Industry

Regardless of widespread male disapproval, certain economic and social factors made women workers an ever-present reality all through the Industrial Revolution. In the early years of that revolution, for example, hiring women proved financially convenient for both employers and women. In those days a majority of female workers labored in New England's growing textile industry. Most often, mill owners found it practical to recruit their employees from farms in the rural areas surrounding the mill towns. There, many farmers were having trouble making ends meet. Thus, they needed everyone in the family to earn at least some money. This included daughters, whose incentive to take jobs in factories is summarized by Cornell University scholar Barbara M. Wertheimer:

Wives were still needed on the farms to raise the children and cook, but daughters could be spared for the mills, work that the young women found vastly preferable to the other option open to most of them: domestic service [i.e., maids and other kinds of servants]. In any event, they viewed millwork as merely an interlude before marriage and family responsibilities.[27]

As time went on, women began taking industrial jobs for other reasons. In some cases, women worked outside the home, including factories and sweatshops, because they had to support, or at least help support, their families.

Mill girls at a Manchester cotton factory leave for dinner. Farm girls often left their homes for jobs in the city in order to help their families make ends meet.

Some were single mothers whose husbands had died or abandoned them. Others were in situations in which the husband was present and working but did not make enough money to pay the rent and bills.

An even more pressing reason for women to seek work in industry emerged during the early to middle nineteenth century. Harriet H. Robinson toiled in the textile mills in Lowell, Massachusetts, from 1834 to 1848.

Several years later she wrote her autobiography, in which she recalled her work experiences. She pointed out that in the mill towns it was common for one or more women in a family to work in the factories to make money to help educate a brother or other male in the household:

> The most prevailing incentive to labor was to secure the means of education for some *male* member

of the family. To make a *gentleman* of a brother or a son, to give him a college education, was the dominant thought in the minds of a great many of the better class of mill girls. I have known more than one to give every cent of her wages, month after month, to her brother, that he might get the education necessary to enter some profession. I have known a mother to work years in this way for her boy. I have known women to educate young men by their earnings, who were not sons or relatives. There are many men now living who were helped to an education by the wages of the early mill girls.[28]

Robinson pointed out still another reason why some women felt compelled to take industrial jobs: Namely, it was the only way a woman could become financially independent. The sad truth for most women, Robinson wrote, was that they had little or no access to money or property in the traditional ways that men did:

At this time a woman had no property rights. A widow could be left without her share of her husband's (or the family) property. . . . A father could make his will without reference to his daughter's share of the inheritance. He usually left her a home on the farm as long as she

Female Coal Miners

A study conducted by Britain's Parliament in 1842 found that several women worked alongside and endured the same appalling working conditions as men in the country's coal mines. One of them, Betty Harris, aged thirty-seven, gave the following testimony:

I was married at 23, and went into a colliery [mine] when I was married. . . . I have a belt round my waist, and a chain passing between my legs, and I go on my hands and feet. The road [tunnel floor] is very steep, and we have to hold by a rope; and when there is no rope, by anything we can catch hold of. There are six women and about six boys and girls in the pit I work in; it is very hard work for a woman. The pit is very wet where I work, and the water comes over our clog-tops always, and I have seen it up to my thighs. . . . I am very tired when I get home at night; I fall asleep sometimes before I get washed. I am not so strong as I was, and cannot stand my work so well as I used to.

Quoted in Internet Modern History Source Book, "Women Miners in the English Coal Pits." www.fordham.edu/halsall/mod/1842womenminers.html.

remained single. A woman was not supposed to be capable of spending her own, or of using other people's money. In Massachusetts, before 1840, a woman could not, legally, be treasurer of her own sewing society, unless some man were responsible for her. The law [did not recognize a] woman as a money-spender. . . . Thus it happened that if a woman did not choose to marry, or, when left a widow, to remarry, she had no choice but to enter one of the few employments open to her [in many cases a factory job], or to become a burden on the charity of some relative.[29]

Low Pay and No Job Security

Although most women who found work in industry were gratified to be employed, they had no illusions that their jobs would make them financially well-off or even comfortable. Throughout the years of the Industrial Revolution it was a simple fact of life that women workers earned very low wages. And usually these were in exchange for a great deal of time and labor.

Moreover, in a number of regions and industries women's wages actually declined over the course of the nineteenth century (while men's wages steadily increased). In the 1830s, for instance, female textile workers in Lowell endured a series of pay cuts that agitated them to go on strike. In the 1850s women who sewed clothes in factories

and sweatshops saw their wages decline, too. Indeed, women were financially exploited particularly badly by sweatshop owners. Of many examples, Jacob Riis recalled that of a woman who barely survived by making paper bags in a New York sweatshop:

> There is scarce a branch of woman's work outside of the home in which wages, long since at low-water mark, have not fallen to the point of actual starvation. A case was brought to my notice recently [of] a widow with two little children [who worked] in an East Side attic, making paper-bags. [She] received only five cents for six hundred of the little three-cornered bags, and her fingers had to be very swift and handle the paste-brush very deftly to bring her earnings up to twenty-five and thirty cents a day.[30]

A few years later, in 1863, female umbrella makers in New York City were in similarly dire straits. Often working from six in the morning till midnight, they made only about eighty cents per day. This prompted a local newspaper to remark: "No class of female operatives . . . have suffered more from a lack of just compensation for their labor."[31]

In addition to the often distressingly low pay, most women industrial laborers endured other hardships and humiliations. They had few or no chances for advancement beyond the most menial positions, for example. (For a long time

Declining wages in the nineteenth century forced some women to strike for better pay, as shown in this illustration of the Lynn, Massachusetts, shoemaker strike in 1860.

there were no female managers in British or American industry.) Furthermore, female workers were frequently fined (had their pay docked) for trivial mistakes made on the job. Riis reported the case of a young woman who made two dollars per week selling various items in a factory outlet store. For the "offense" of sitting down a couple of times during her long shift, she was fined sixty cents, almost a third of her weekly wage. "The law requiring seats for sales women, generally ignored, was obeyed faithfully in this establishment," Riis wrote. "The seats were there, but the girls were fined when found using them."[32]

Women workers could also be fired on a mere whim by a manager or other boss. Sometimes this happened because a worker broke a rule. But just as often women were let go because they were getting older and managers felt that younger replacements would be more productive. In the 1850s, the owner of an American textile mill stated: "I regard my work-people just as I regard my machinery. When my machines get old and useless, I reject them and get new [ones], and these people are part of my machinery."[33]

In the New England mills, moreover, women were subjected to workplace

Her First Day in a Sweatshop

One of the survivors of the infamous Triangle Shirtwaist factory fire, Rose Cohen, later recalled her first day in the sweatshop when she was still in her teens.

All day I took my finished [sewing] work and laid it on the boss's table. He would glance at the clock and give me other work. Before the day was over I knew that this was a "piece work shop," that there were four machines and sixteen people were working. I also knew that I had done almost as much work as "the grownup girls" and that they did not like me. . . . Seven o'clock came and everyone worked on. I wanted to [go home]. But I had not the courage to stand up alone. . . . My neck felt stiff and my back ached. I wished there were a back to my chair so that I could rest against it a little. When the people began to go home it seemed to me that it had been night a long time. The next morning when I came into the shop at seven o'clock, I saw at once that all the people were there and working steadily as if they had been at work a long while.

Rose Cohen, "My First Job," Triangle Factory Fire. www .ilr.cornell.edu/trianglefire/texts/stein_ootss/ootss_rc.ht ml?location=Sweatshops+and+Strikes.

intimidation and blackmail if they wanted to leave their jobs. Employers set up a system in which women wanting to quit had to get what amounted to an honorable discharge. To earn a discharge, she had to have worked at the mill for at least a year and she was expected to give two weeks' notice. If she left without fulfilling these conditions, she found herself blacklisted in every mill town in the region and thereby unable to find another job.

The Call of the Factory Bell

To make matters worse, those women who stayed in their factory and sweatshop jobs encountered adverse working conditions. There were the long hours, dim lighting, and poor ventilation common to most industrial settings, of course. There were also the standard dangers, such as getting their hair, skirts, or hands caught in machinery and the threat of fire or the building collapsing.

A number of factories partially or fully collapsed during the nineteenth century. One of the worst instances in the United States took place in January 1860 when the five-story Pemberton textile mill in Lawrence, Massachusetts, suddenly caved in. Of the estimated 90 to 145 killed and more than 160 injured, most were young women.

In addition, most of the industrial jobs women held in that era were extremely regimented. In the early 1800s, female mill workers in New England were assaulted by a series of loud factory bells that directed their behavior at all hours of the day and night. One bell sounded at 4:00 or 4:30 A.M., awakening those young women who lived in dormitories situated beside the mills. Another bell marked the beginning of work at 5:00 or 5:30. There were also bells to signal the start and end of breakfast and lunch, quitting time at 7:00 or 7:30 P.M., and bedtime, usually at 10:00. Not surprisingly, the workers became resentful of this strictly controlled schedule. And they composed songs and poems of lament. One went:

> It was morning, and the factory bell
> Had sent forth its early call,
> And many a weary one was there,
> Within the dull factory wall.
> And amidst the clashing noise and din
> Of the ever beating loom,
> Stood a fair young girl with throbbing brow
> Working her way to the tomb.[34]

Although the working conditions of women in textile mills were unpleasant and at times unjust, women in other industries had it even worse. An article

The ruins of the Pemberton Mill after the building caved in. Many women in factory jobs encountered adverse working conditions, including factory collapses.

published in New York's *Daily Tribune* in 1845 exposed the unenviable plight of female artificial-flower makers in that city, saying in part:

[Their pitiful salaries] will barely serve to furnish them the scantiest [tiniest] and poorest food, which from the [job's] monotony and its unhealthy quality induces disgust, loathing, and disease. . . . Their [bodies] are bent by incessant and stooping toil, their health destroyed by want [lack] of rest and proper exercise, and their minds . . . stunted, brutalized, and destroyed over their monotonous tasks.[35]

Despite occasional bursts of outrage like this one, little or nothing was done at the time to alleviate women's deplorable workplace situations. It took nearly another century for labor strikes, disasters like the Triangle Shirtwaist fire, changing social customs, and new, more enlightened laws to make women's industrial work acceptably safe and fair.

Chapter Four

CHILD LABOR IN INDUSTRY

Child labor existed in one form or another across the world long before the advent of the Industrial Revolution. But the use of children as full-time workers expanded and became highly organized during the machine age. This happened in part because industrial employers realized that they could pay children far less than adults. Furthermore, children could operate many of the same machines that adults could, especially in textile mills; so companies could increase their profit margins by filling many of their industrial jobs with children. As one modern observer puts it:

The textile machines themselves played a large part in part in encouraging the use of child labor. [Spinning jennies and other early textile] machines were so easy to operate that unskilled children could easily [do so]. Moreover, centralized manufacturing with machines and children under the watchful eye of an adult overseer provided a very economical method of production.[36]

Most mill owners and other employers during that period did not see anything wrong with hiring children to work long hours in dreary, often dangerous factories. And these bosses typically used various arguments to rationalize this practice. One of the more common ones was that many poor families needed their children to work in order to survive. The owners also claimed they were only meeting this demand by supplying the needed jobs. Another frequently cited rationale was that the children were "free agents."

Children working in a twine factory in New York City in the 1870s. Child labor was a way for factory owners to cut labor costs because they could pay children less.

That is, like their parents, they had the mental capacity to decide what they should do with their lives, including if and where they should work.

British politician and labor reformer Michael T. Sadler (1780–1835) strongly disagreed with this view. "Free agents!" he thundered in a speech delivered to Parliament in 1832.

The idea of treating children, and especially the children of [the] poor imprisoned in factories, as free agents, is too absurd [to take seriously]. The protection of poor children and young persons from these hardships and cruelties . . . has [long] been held [to be] one of the first and most important duties of every Christian legislature.[37]

Sadler felt so strongly that child labor practices should be reformed that he led a government investigation of the problem. He interviewed many former child laborers, factory overseers, and others involved in industry. This material provides modern studies of the Industrial Revolution with a crucial, revealing window into child labor conditions during that era.

Jobs Done by Children

Sadler's investigation and its findings focused on child labor in Britain. However, the same conditions experienced by children in industry there prevailed

Young boys sit in rows in front of a coal breaker, picking out slate in an anthracite mine in Pennsylvania. Children worked in a wide range of industrial jobs in the 1800s.

in France, the United States, and other rapidly industrializing countries. And the jobs performed by children in factories and other industrial workplaces were largely the same in all these nations.

The large proportion of children working in textile mills was universal, for instance. In 1788, when Britain was just beginning to industrialize, an estimated two-thirds of the workers in its mills were younger than eighteen. Later, in 1835, a survey found that the proportion of children in British mills was smaller but was still a hefty 43 percent. The United States followed Britain's lead. Most of the workers in the first American textile mill, in Rhode Island (in 1790), were children between the ages of seven and twelve. By 1830, 55 percent of all mill workers in that state were children.

Children worked in a wide range of other industries as well. Large numbers of young boys labored long hours in coal mines. Workers younger than eighteen were also prominent in shipyards, iron foundries, glassworks, and sweatshops. In addition, some children toiled along the margins of the industrial sector, sifting through its refuse. In Britain they were called mud larks. Often as young as seven or eight, they swarmed over the grounds on the edges of shipyards, coal mines, factories, and even the sewers. Desperately they searched for nails, pieces of scrap metal and rope, lumps of coal and wood, and any other discarded remnants of the manufacturing process that could be sold for a few pennies.

The Sad Lives of Mud Larks

Mud larks were children who scavenged through industrial refuse in hopes of finding discarded items they could sell. Nineteenth-century British journalist Henry Mayhew observed and interviewed some of them. "These poor creatures," he said, "are often the most deplorable in their appearance of any[one] I have met with. . . . They are scarcely covered by the [rags] that serve them for clothing. Their bodies are grimed [filthy] and their torn garments stiffened up like boards with dirt." Mayhew interviewed a single London mother who was too ill to work and had to rely on her nine-year-old son, a mud lark, to support them. Despite their grinding poverty, "he never complained," she said, "and assured me that one day God would see us cared for."

Quoted in Deborah Cadbury, *Dreams of Iron and Steel: Seven Wonders of the Nineteenth Century*. New York: Fourth Estate, 2004, pp. 119–20.

Long Shifts, Little Rest

Inside the factories, meanwhile, the daily routines of child laborers were no less difficult and unrewarding. Owners and their managers and overseers typically forced the children to work extremely long hours by today's standards. A former British child mill worker, Elizabeth Bentley, who was interviewed by Sadler in 1832, recalled:

> I worked from five in the morning till nine at night. I lived two miles [3.2km] from the mill. We had no clock. If I had been too late at the mill, I would have been quartered. I mean that if I had been a quarter of an hour too late, a half an hour would have been taken off [my pay]. I only got a penny an hour, and they would have taken a half-penny.[38]

Another former child mill worker, Frank Forrest, wrote in 1850:

> In reality there were no regular hours. Masters and managers did with us as they liked. The clocks in the factories were often put forward in the morning and back at night. Though this was known amongst the hands [workers], we were afraid to speak, and a workman then was afraid to carry a watch.[39]

Some bosses found that they could get the children to work even longer hours by forcing them to sleep several nights a week in the mills. In such cases, the children were sometimes obliged to work one shift after another with extremely little sleep between shifts. In 1832 former child laborer David Bywater told Sadler's committee:

> We started at one o'clock on Monday morning, and then we went on again till eight o'clock, at breakfast time; then we had [a break of] half an hour; and then we went on till twelve o'clock, and had half an hour [and] then we stopped at half past eleven [for] an hour and a half. . . . And then we went on again till breakfast time, when we had half an hour; and then we went on again till twelve o'clock, at dinner time, and then we had an hour; and then we stopped at five o'clock again on Tuesday afternoon for half an hour for drinking; then we went on till past eleven, and then we gave over till five o'clock on Wednesday morning. . . . [In the few hours we could catch some sleep] we slept in the mill.[40]

Physical Decline and Accidents

Long hours were only one of many hardships encountered by child industrial workers. The work itself was strenuous and repetitious and over time took a toll on many young bodies. One concerned observer, Samuel Smith, a physician in the British industrial town of Leeds, stated in the 1830s:

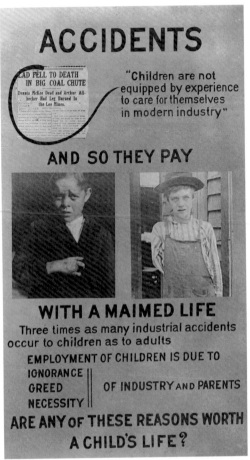

A poster shows child laborers maimed in industrial accidents, advocating that children not work in factories because accidents happened often in industrial workplaces.

Long continued standing has . . . a very injurious effect upon the ankles. But the principal effects which I have seen produced in this way have been upon the knees. By long continued standing the knees become so weak that they turn inwards, producing that deformity which is called "knock-knees" and I have sometimes seen it so striking, that the individual has actually lost twelve inches of his height by it.[41]

The problem of "knock-knees" was also addressed by Hannah Brown, one of the young textile workers whom Sadler interviewed:

Question: How early did you begin to work in mills?
Answer: At nine years old.

Question: What hours did you work?
Answer: I began at six o'clock, and worked till nine at night. . . .

Question: Did this work affect your limbs?
Answer: Yes, I felt a great deal of pain in my legs.

Question: Did it begin to produce deformity in any of your limbs?
Answer: Yes; both my knees are rather turned in.[42]

Sometimes the physical problems suffered by children in industrial workplaces were the results of accidents. Lost fingers and partial scalpings, as hands and hair got caught in machines, were not uncommon. Worst of all was when a child's entire body was drawn into a large machine. Of the surviving accounts of such mishaps, a particularly disturbing one reads:

A girl named Mary Richards, who was . . . not quite ten years of age, attended a [machine], below which, and about a foot from the floor, was a horizontal shaft, by which the [machine gears] above were turned. It happened one evening, when her apron was caught by the shaft. In an instant the poor girl was drawn by an irresistible force and dashed on the floor. She uttered the most heart-rending shrieks! [A fellow worker] saw her whirled round and round with the shaft. He heard the bones of her arms, legs, thighs, etc. successively snap asunder, crushed . . . as the machinery whirled her round, and drew tighter and tighter her body within the works. Her blood was scattered over the [machine] and streamed upon the floor. . . . When she was [removed from the machine], every bone was found broken [and] her head [was] dreadfully crushed. She was carried off quite lifeless.[43]

Punishments and Abuse

Some of the other physical problems child workers suffered were the result of deliberate physical abuse. Harsh punishments, even for trivial offenses, were common both in Britain and the United States. For example, children who worked long hours sometimes dozed off at their work stations. The penalty for this "crime" was to plunge the offender head first into a barrel of water. Another routine punishment was

Memories of a Disabled Child Laborer

Long hours of factory labor often caused physical deformities in children. William Dodd worked as a child laborer in Britain. In 1841 the adult Dodd wrote a book titled A Narrative of a Factory Cripple. *Describing one of the consequences of his factory work, he said:*

[I]n] the spring of 1840, I began to feel some painful symptoms in my right wrist, arising from the general weakness of my joints, brought on in the factories. The swelling and pain increased.

The wrist eventually measured twelve inches round and I was worn down to a mere skeleton. I entered St. Thomas's Hospital and on 18th July, I underwent the operation. The hand being taken off a little below the elbow. On dissection, the bones of the forearm presented a very curious appearance, something similar to an empty honeycomb, the marrow having totally disappeared.

Quoted in Spartacus Educational: The Industrial Revolution, "Child Labor: Physical Deformities." www.spartacus .schoolnet.co.uk/IRdeformities.htm.

called weighting. An overseer attached heavy iron bars to a child's torso and forced him or her to walk back and forth across the factory floor for half an hour, an hour, or more.

Perhaps the most common punishment was beating. This was done variously by hands, belts, canes, sticks, whips, and other means. One victim, Sarah Carpenter, told a British newspa-

Deliberate physical abuse was common for working children. Factory foremen frequently beat the children who worked for them.

per in 1849 how her overseer, William Hughes, had noticed that her machine had stopped. Though this was not her fault, she said,

Hughes starting beating me with a stick, and when he had done I told him I would let my mother know. He then went out and fetched the master [mill manager] in to me. The master started beating me with a stick over the head till it was full of lumps and bled. My head was so bad that I could not sleep for a long time, and I [have] never been a sound sleeper since.[44]

Another recollection of beatings carried out by factory overseers was recorded by a former British child laborer named Samuel Fielden in 1887:

Woe be to the child who shall be behind in doing its allotted work. The machine will be started and the poor child's fingers will be bruised and skinned with the revolving spools. While the children try to catch up to their comrades . . . the brutal [overseer] will frequently beat them unmercifully, and I have frequently seen them strike the children, knocking them off their stools and sending them spinning several feet on the greasy floor.[45]

Sadly, it was very difficult, as well as risky, for child industrial workers to report the abuses they suffered on the job. Former British child laborer John Birley made the following statement as an adult in 1849:

Frank [the sadistic son of the mill's owner] once beat me till he frightened himself. He thought he had killed me. He had struck me on the temples and knocked me [unconscious]. My elbow was broken. I bear the marks, and suffer pain from it to this day. . . . I was determined to let the [authorities] know the treatment we [children] had, and I wrote a letter . . . and put it into the Tydeswell Post Office. It was broken open and given to [the factory owner]. He beat us with a knob-stick till we could scarcely crawl. Sometime after this three [factory inspectors] came down from London. But before we were examined we were washed and cleaned up and ordered to tell them we liked working at the mill and were well treated. [The owner] and his sons were in the room at the time. They asked us questions about our treatment, which we answered as we had been told, not daring to do any other, knowing what would happen if we told them the truth.[46]

Considering such abuses, in addition to the long hours and adverse working conditions the children endured, it is hardly surprising that some children tried to escape. This is one reason why locks, gates, and fences were installed in

Eyewitness to Abuse

The full extent of the child abuse in British and American factories during the Industrial Revolution will likely never be known. But there is extensive surviving eyewitness testimony to beatings and numerous other severe punishments of child workers. Some children were actually killed on the job. According to a statement given to a newspaper in 1849 by former British child laborer Sarah Carpenter:

There was a young woman, Sarah Goodling, who was [feeling sick] and so she stopped her machine. James Birch, the over[seer] knocked her to the floor. She got up as well as she could. He knocked her down again. Then she was carried to the apprentice house. Her bedfellow found her dead in bed. There was another called Mary. She knocked her food can down on the floor. The master, Mr. Newton, kicked her where he should not do, and it caused her to wear away till she died. There was another, Caroline Thompson. They beat her till she went out of her mind.

Quoted in Spartacus Educational: The Industrial Revolution, "Child Labor: Punishment in Factories." www.spartacus.schoolnet.co.uk/IRpunishments.htm.

---

factories during that era. Some children were actually shackled in chains to prevent them from leaving their posts and running away. According to one eyewitness, Robert Blincoe:

The blacksmith had the task of riveting irons upon any of the apprentices, whom the master ordered. These irons were very much like the irons usually put upon felons [criminals]. Even young women, if they were suspected of intending to run away, had irons riveted on their ankles, and reaching by long links and rings up to the hips, and in these they were compelled to walk to and fro from the mill to work and to sleep.[47]

Reforms Slow in Coming

The long hours, physical decline, horrific accidents, beatings, and other abuses suffered by children in industrial workplaces were widely known in Britain, the United States, and other industrialized nations. But for a long time attempts to eliminate such abuses were only minimally successful. Thanks in large part to Sadler's investigation, Britain's Parliament passed the Factory Acts in 1833 and 1834. These banned children younger than nine from working and made it illegal for children under eighteen to work more than twelve hours a day.

Yet despite these and other periodic reforms, child labor continued well into the twentieth century in Britain. The same was true in the United States. There, Congress did not pass the first law banning child labor until 1916. Moreover, the law was not widely enforced until the 1930s. Thus, today's strict laws protecting children from inhumane labor practices and workplace abuses are very recent developments.

Chapter Five

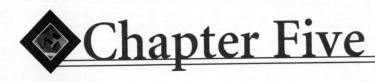

Immigrant Industrial Workers

It was clear from the country's beginnings that the United States had been and would likely long remain a nation of immigrants. J. Hector St. John de Crèvecoeur (1735–1813), an American patriot who had moved from France to New York before the American Revolution, summed it up well. In his *Letters from an American Farmer,* penned in 1782, he commented on the diversity of the immigrants who had settled in America and correctly recognized that this diversity was good for the country:

What then is the American, this new man? He is either a European, or the descendant of a European, hence that strange mixture of blood, which you will find in no other country. I could point out to you a family whose grandfather was an Englishman, whose wife was Dutch, whose son married a French woman, and whose present four sons have now four wives of different nations. *He* is an American, who, leaving behind him all his ancient prejudices and manners, receives new ones from the new mode of life he has embraced. . . . Here individuals of all nations are melted into a new race of men, whose labors and posterity will one day cause great changes in the world.[48]

When de Crèvecoeur wrote these words, he was unable to foresee the nature of the "new mode of life" that later immigrants would encounter in America. During the late 1700s and early 1800s, the Industrial Revolution gradually spread from Britain to the United States. As time went on, immigrants filled a large proportion of the resulting jobs in factories, mines, sweatshops, and other industrial workplaces. In fact, some scholars suggest that the increasing number of immigrants who came to America in the nineteenth century introduced a large new workforce. And the availability of that workforce, made up of people who were willing to work long hours for low pay, helped to stimulate the expansion of the U.S. factory system.

Successive Waves of Immigrants

Indeed, the three major waves of immigration in that era coincided with the

Immigrants from Europe arrive at a U.S. port in the 1800s. New immigrants filled a large proportion of industrial jobs.

Immigrants Made America Strong

In 1782, in his Letters from an American Farmer, *French American writer J. Hector St. John de Crèvecoeur recognized the strength America could draw from its wide range of immigrants. He also remarked how eager they were to work in American industries.*

Americans are the western pilgrims, who are carrying along with them that great mass of arts, sciences, vigor, and industry which began long since in the east; they will finish the great circle. The Americans were once scattered all over Europe; here they are incorporated into one of the finest systems of population which has ever appeared, and which will hereafter become distinct by the power of the different climates they inhabit. The American ought therefore to love this country much better than that wherein either he or his forefathers were born. Here the rewards of his industry follow with equal steps the progress of his labor.

Quoted in Internet Modern History Source Book, "What Is an American?" www.fordham.edu/halsall/mod/crevecour2.html.

steady emergence of America as an industrial giant. The first wave occurred between 1815 and 1865, when more than 5 million immigrants came. Of these, many were Irish. About 100,000 Irish moved to the United States in 1846 alone, in this case to escape the infamous potato famine that ravaged their homeland. By 1854, 2 million Irish, roughly a quarter of Ireland's entire population, had immigrated to America. Large numbers of the newcomers took jobs in factories, mines, and other industrial workplaces. Of the other immigrants who came during this period, more than a million were Germans, of whom 10,000 were coal miners. About 40,000 British coal miners arrived, too, mainly in the 1850s. (Half of the American miners in that era had been born outside the United States.)

The second big wave of immigration took place between 1865 and 1890. This time about 10 million people arrived. Most of them, as before, were from northern Europe, including Britain, Ireland, Germany, and the Scandinavian countries. As might be expected, the majority of these immigrants settled in the eastern portion of the United States. Meanwhile, in the western portion, more than 100,000 Chinese immigrants arrived and found work constructing the railroad lines then expanding rapidly through that region. The Chinese also worked in textile mills and garment sweatshops. By 1880 about 25 percent of

California's entire workforce was Chinese. At the same time, many Mexicans moved northward into the American Southwest.

The third major wave of immigrants into the United States, numbering about 15 million, occurred between 1890 and 1914. This time most came from the Mediterranean countries and eastern Europe. There were many Italians, Greeks, Romanians, Serbs, Poles, and Jews, among others. They worked in a wide range of industries, including the railroads, meatpacking plants, steel mills, and the newly emerging auto plants. They also worked in sweatshops along with members of nearly every other immigrant and ethnic group. In 1907 Jacob Riis observed:

[There is a] great diversity of foreign immigrants among New York workers. One may find for the asking an Italian, a German, a French, African, Spanish, Bohemian, Russian, Scandinavian, Jewish, and Chinese colony. Even the Arab . . . has his exclusive preserves at the lower end of Washington Street.[49]

Irish families stand outside an emigrant office, hoping to move to America in 1845. The Irish composed the majority of the first wave of immigrants entering the United States between 1815 and 1865.

Many Entry-Level Jobs

The individuals who owned factories, sweatshops, railroads, and other industrial concerns took advantage of the steady infusion of immigrants into the workforce. A majority of the available industrial jobs required few or no special skills, so in most cases a person could be quickly trained to do a simple, repetitive step in a manufacturing process. These workers could be paid relatively little for their labor.

As a result, the vast majority of immigrants, especially after 1880, were categorized as unskilled laborers. By 1907, 81 percent of the unskilled workers in Andrew Carnegie's steel company were immigrants from eastern Europe. Indeed, many immigrants settled in the Pittsburgh area exactly because it was where most of the steel industry jobs were located. Similarly, various groups of immigrants migrated to other key cities known for certain kinds of industry;

Immigrants wait outside Castle Garden in New York for job offers. Employers found a ready pool of new labor with each fresh wave of immigrants.

Immigrants Are Drawn to Cities

University of Wisconsin scholar Stanley K. Schultz here attempts to explain why so many of the foreign immigrants who arrived in America during the Industrial Revolution settled in cities.

Many immigrants came to America with little money to buy farms or expensive farming equipment. Others settled in cities because American agriculture was far different from what most had been accustomed to in Europe. Some, including many Slavs, simply came to America too late to acquire free or cheap land. Others moved to cities for different reasons. Many Irish opted for an urban life because they associated farming with the English landlords who had persecuted Irish tenant farmers. Immigrants, particularly Jews, settled in urban areas because their forebears had already established vibrant cultural, religious, and educational institutions throughout many of the nation's largest cities.

Stanley K. Schultz, "Foreign Immigrants in Industrial America," American History 102. http://us.history.wisc.edu/hist102/lectures/lecture08.html.

these included Chicago for meatpacking; Lowell, Massachusetts, for textiles; and Detroit for automaking. Poles became particularly prominent in the auto industry. By 1910 almost thirty-six thousand Polish immigrants lived and worked in Detroit. That city and its auto plants also absorbed thirty thousand Italians, twenty thousand Russians, eleven thousand Hungarians, nine thousand Yugoslavians, and six thousand Greeks.

Another reason why so many immigrants made low wages was because, as newcomers, most were willing to start at the bottom and take entry-level jobs. Thus, it was typical for each new wave of immigrants to take over the lowest-paying jobs in an industry. A clear example was the case of the numerous textile mills in nineteenth-century Lowell. In the 1850s Irish immigrants were hired for most of the entry-level positions. Soon afterward, in the 1860s and 1870s, newly arrived French Canadians replaced many Irish in these jobs. (The population of French Canadians in Lowell increased from two thousand in 1870 to fourteen thousand in 1905.) The next wave of immigrants, including Poles and Greeks, took the lowest-paying jobs in Lowell's mills between 1890 and 1910. By that time, nearly all of the workers in these facilities, at every pay level, were from foreign lands; only 10 percent were native born.

Meanwhile, Pennsylvania's coal mines were thriving thanks to immigrants who eagerly filled every opening they could find. Many of the Irish, English, Scots, Germans, and others who took these jobs had been coal miners in their native lands. So in many cases mining was all they knew. And they were willing to work for low wages for the sake of tradition and continuity in addition to the opportunity to have steady work.

Immigrant Inventers

Although the majority of immigrants who came to America during the Industrial Revolution were unskilled, menial laborers, a few were highly educated and extremely skilled. For example, several inventors and scientists who moved to the United States from abroad became key figures in industry and business. In fact, without these immigrants the American Industrial Revolution would likely have been less expansive and successful.

For example, one of the great breakthroughs in American industry was the replacement of steam with electricity as the main industrial power source. (The new technology soon spread to many other parts of the globe). Several inventors contributed to the development of electrical currents and circuits. One of the most crucial, however, was Croatian-born Nikola Tesla (1856–1943). He arrived in the United States in 1884 and in the 1890s developed motors that ran on alternating current. These significantly increased the distances that electricity could be transmitted. And factories and businesses across America rapidly made the transi-

tion from steam and other older, less efficient and less reliable energy sources.

No less impressive were the contributions of other immigrant inventors. One of the most famous was Scottish-born Alexander Graham Bell (1847–1922), who moved to the United States in the 1870s. In that same decade he developed the telephone, which revolutionized communications, including those in industry and business.

Croatian-born inventor Nikola Tesla helped develop electrical currents and circuits. He developed motors that ran on alternating current (AC), which increased the distances that electricity could be transmitted.

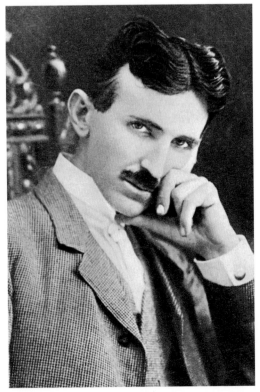

A Giant of the Printing Industry

German-born Ottmar Mergenthaler was one of several examples of an immigrant who revolutionized an industry and thereby helped America become more prosperous. The Literary Heritage Project in Baltimore, where he lived and worked, provides this synopsis of his achievements.

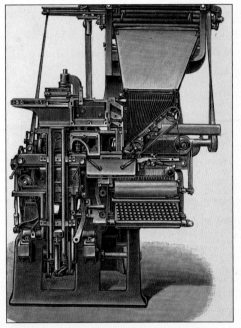

Ottmar Mergenthaler invented the Linotype, which revolutionized the printing industry.

Ottmar Mergenthaler . . . invented the Linotype—which enabled printers to create and assemble type far faster than could have been done previously. And that meant that publishers could print books, newspapers, magazines, and other work much faster than before. . . . By 1904, there were 10,000 Linotypes in use; by 1954, the centennial of Mergenthaler's birth, that number had skyrocketed to 100,000. . . . [His son], Herman Mergenthaler, said this about his father: "The history of printing, which some say dates back to [the year] 868, is crowded with the names of many men who have made extraordinary contributions to it. But two men—two giants—stand out in bold relief. They are Johann Gutenberg [inventor of the printing press] and Ottmar Mergenthaler."

Quoted in Baltimore Literary Heritage Project, "Ottmar Mergenthaler." http://baltimoreauthors.ubalt.edu/writers/ottomergenthaler.htm.

In the following decade a German immigrant named Ottmar Mergenthaler (1854–1899) invented the Linotype machine. It vastly improved the printing process, which in turn expanded the printing industry and increased the number of newspapers across America and the world. Renowned American-born inventor Thomas Edison called Mergenthaler's machine the "eighth wonder of the world."[50]

Challenges Faced by Immigrant Workers

Whether their achievements in American industry were big or small, nearly all immigrant workers faced certain challenges, both before and after they arrived in the United States. The first major obstacle to overcome was getting to the so-called land of opportunity in the first place. Many would-be American workers were poor peasants who lived in Europe's more remote rural areas. They first had to find practical ways to move their families to port cities along Mediterranean or Atlantic coasts. Then they had to cross the vast Atlantic Ocean safely and for a reasonable price. After arriving in the United States, they had to find some means of getting to various American cities and towns, some located hundreds of miles inland. Fortunately for these foreign workers, the Industrial Revolution had already provided relatively new forms of transportation that overcame all of these travel challenges. According to scholar Sukkoo Kim:

> Advances in internal transportation due to railroads provided easy access to major ports for most European populations. Second, the advances in steamship technology made the trans-Atlantic travel shorter, safer, and easier to get in and out of secondary ports in the Mediterranean. Third, the passenger costs relative to per capita income fell significantly between 1820 and 1860. . . . Most

immigrants entered the United States through New York and used domestic transportation networks to reach their intended destinations. Between 1850 and 1914, 70% of immigrants arrived via the ports in New York and many immigrants moved immediately from the port of entry to internal destinations.[51]

Having arrived in the United States, most immigrants who sought jobs in various industries were able to find them. This was partly because American industry was in a rapid expansion phase during the late 1800s and new jobs were always being created. Also, most immigrants were willing to work for low wages, at least for a few years.

However, foreign-born workers soon found that there were certain drawbacks to their working and living in America. One was that it was risky to complain to the boss about one's working conditions, no matter how adverse or substandard they might be. Employers were well aware that they could easily find another immigrant to take the same job. Complainers were usually fired. During the nineteenth century, most immigrants were also afraid to address workplace issues by joining unions. A majority of the country's inhabitants still saw unions as un-American. Few immigrants were willing to take the chance of earning that negative label. After all, many of them viewed becoming an American as a great privilege and even as their life's dream.

Northern European immigrants recruit help in getting to the American Midwest. Immigrant workers faced many challenges in getting to their end destinations.

Prejudice and Blending In

Impeding this goal of becoming an American to one degree or another was the larger societal reality of anti-immigrant sentiments among many native-born Americans. Millions of the latter looked on immigrants with suspicion. Some resented the idea of foreigners taking jobs that might otherwise go to natives. Others worried that immigrants would place their loyalties to their home countries above loyalty to America, especially in wartime. Still others had religious or racial biases against certain immigrants.

Faced with this diverse array of prejudices, a majority of immigrant workers sought to assimilate, or blend into, American society as much as possible. Most learned English, even if they spoke it with a noticeable accent. They also raised their children, many of whom were born in the United States, to become proud Americans. Large numbers in this second generation worked in the same factories and other workplaces as their parents. But they spoke English without an accent and blended into society in ways their parents could not. This reinforced the image of America as a "melting pot," an idea that achieved wide popularity in the early 1900s. The great American journalist and political commentator Walter Lippmann recognized this reality and remarked in 1914:

We are all of us immigrants spiritually. We are all of us immigrants in the industrial world, and we have no authority to lean upon. We are an uprooted people, newly arrived. . . . As a nation we have all the vulgarity that goes with that, all the scattering of soul. The modern man is not yet settled in his world. It is strange to him, terrifying, alluring, and incomprehensibly big.[52]

Lippmann saw that the Industrial Revolution had remade the world, including America. The onrush of industry and technology had in a sense created a new, fast-paced society. In his view, everyone, whether native or foreign born, was a new arrival in that society and was still trying to adjust. So it made sense for all, regardless of background, to get along for the greater good. This sentiment was prophetic. As American industry continued to expand during the twentieth century, some of the children and grandchildren of immigrants became factory owners and managers themselves. And the greater good was indeed achieved as the United States became an economic powerhouse and the world's superpower.

Chapter Six

ORGANIZED LABOR AND INDUSTRY

During the Industrial Revolution, workers in Britain, the United States, and other industrializing countries encountered numerous work-related problems. Among others, these included long hours, low wages, dirty and unsafe working conditions, and abusive treatment by bosses and overseers. For a long time there was little that most ordinary workers could do to address and eliminate such ills. More often than not both government and society tended to side with industry. After all, the manufacturing sector, which had been transformed by machines, provided millions of jobs, increased trade revenues, and made a nation's overall economy strong. Considering these facts, the needs and complaints of mostly impoverished workers, who had no political voice, seemed secondary to the greater good.

Nevertheless, as time went on more and more industrial workers saw that there was at least some strength in numbers. Little by little they formed labor organizations, most often called unions, dedicated to lobbying or negotiating for improved working conditions. These groups also organized strikes (organized work stoppages) to put pressure on employers to improve working conditions. Thus, in many ways the formation of unions (often called trade unions) was a reaction to, or by-product of, large-scale industrialization. As John Mitchell, a major nineteenth-century American union organizer, bluntly put it:

No one can understand the true nature of trade unionism without understanding the Industrial Revolution and what it has accomplished. The history of mankind has been more virtually affected by changes in its machines and its methods of doing business than by any action or counsel of statesmen or philosophers. What we call the modern world, with its huge populations, its giant cities, its . . . contrasts of wealth and poverty, this great, whirling, restless civilization, with all its vexing problems, is the offspring merely of changed methods of producing wealth. The condition of workmen in the textile and other factories was incredibly bad. [So industrial workers were forced to organize to better their situations.][53]

The efforts of union organizers like Mitchell eventually produced full-blown labor movements in various countries. The U.S. movement was one of the largest and most influential. In many ways it mirrored what happened in several other industrialized countries.

Arguments Against Organized Labor

Before the American labor movement developed during the Industrial Revolution, the concept of workers banding together against their employers was widely viewed as harmful to society. Indeed, many Americans saw organized labor unions as a threat to democracy. There was fear that union members might be more concerned with their own problems than with the nation's needs. Likewise, union strikes and demands might undermine the existing econom-

ic and political systems, including the growing industrial sector that had made the United States strong.

Moreover, most successful businessmen opposed organized labor on a more personal level. The industrialists who owned the factories, along with major merchants and traders who bought and sold their manufactured goods, worried that unions would interfere with free markets. This might significantly reduce company profits and private fortunes.

Also, many of these mainly upper-class individuals insisted that there was no need for unions in the first place. According to this view, conditions in the factories were not as bad as workers claimed they were. One antiunionist stated:

The laboring man in this bounteous and hospitable country has no ground for complaint. Elsewhere he is a creature of circumstance, which is that of abject depression. Under the government of this nation, the effort is to elevate the standard of the human race and not to degrade it. In all other nations it is the reverse. What, therefore, has the laborer to complain of in America? By inciting strikes and encouraging discontent, he stands in the way of the elevation of his race and of mankind.[54]

Making Unions Legal

For these and other reasons, labor unions were illegal in the United States before 1842. They were seen as criminal conspira-

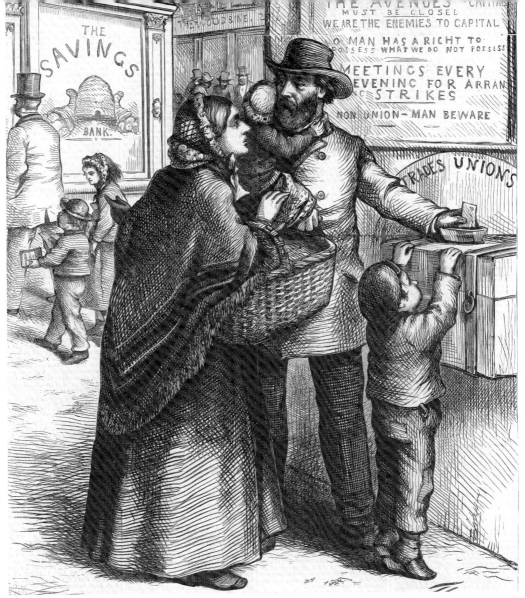

An anti-union illustration shows a working man voting to join a trade union. The sign above the ballot box includes subtle anti-union messages. Behind them, a well-dressed anti-union man walks into a savings bank. During this time, many Americans viewed labor unions as harmful to society.

cies, and their leaders were prosecuted. A case in point—the one that brought about some initial reform—was a court decision that became known as *Commonwealth v. Hunt*. In 1839 a small Boston union of boot makers called a strike to protest the hiring of nonunion workers by any local boot-making factories or workshops. The group's leaders, including John Hunt, were arrested and charged with conspiracy.

Strikers assail the men guarding Carnegie Steel Works in 1892. In 1842 a court decision ruled that unions were legal and union members could go on strike as long as they were not involved in anything criminal or illegal while doing so.

However, the case eventually went to the Massachusetts Supreme Court. In 1842 the chief justice, Lemuel Shaw, ruled that unions *were* legal. Furthermore, union members could go on strike as long as they did not participate in any criminal or other illegal activities while doing so.

The decision paved the way, to some degree, for organized labor in the country. However, factory owners, police, and judges in other states did not automatically accept Shaw's reasoning or authority. And no legal protection for unions was enacted on a national level until the 1930s. Throughout the remainder of the 1800s, therefore, many individual industries and local authorities across the country continued to treat union organizers as troublemakers and even as criminals.

In addition, when worker-friendly laws were occasionally passed in various states before the 1850s, factory owners and other employers usually found ways to evade them. During that period, for example, several small groups of workers pressed for a ten-hour workday. (Twelve-to fourteen-hour days were then the norm.) Collectively, these efforts became informally known as the ten-hour movement. When a few states passed laws mandating ten-hour workdays (New Hampshire in 1847, Pennsylvania in 1848, and Ohio in 1852), industrial bosses found convenient legal loopholes to exploit. One allowed them to make separate contracts with individual workers who were willing to work more than ten hours. When a majority of workers in a factory had signed such contracts, those without contracts were fired; that way the factory continued to operate for fourteen or more hours each day in spite of the ten-hour laws.

Organized Labor Expands

Thus, there was a real need for organized labor to bring about more meaningful reforms by gaining concessions from industry. But this goal took a long time and the concerted efforts of thousands of dedicated, courageous individuals to achieve. The main reason was that so-called organized labor was not yet nearly as organized as it needed to be. Before the 1860s, unions were generally small groups confined to individual towns or local regions. They lacked competent direction, long-term planning,

Labor Unions Are Not Conspiracies

Massachusetts Supreme Court chief justice Lemuel Shaw's 1842 ruling that labor unions were legal, rather than criminal conspiracies, included a clear definition of what a conspiracy is, a view widely adopted by later judges. Shaw stated in part:

A conspiracy must be a combination of two or more persons, by some concerted action, to accomplish some criminal or unlawful purpose, or to accomplish some purpose . . . by criminal or unlawful means. . . . We think, therefore, that associations may be entered into, the object of which is to adopt measures that may have a tendency to impoverish another, that is, to diminish his gains and profits, and so far from being criminal or unlawful, the object [as in the case of unions versus industry] may be highly meritorious [admirable] and public spirited.

Quoted in Harold S. Roberts, *Roberts' Dictionary of Industrial Relations.* Arlington, VA: BNA, 1994, p. 130.

and effective coordination of members and their activities. As a result, when they did stage strikes, these were largely unsuccessful.

A hopeful step forward was the formation of the Order of the Knights of Crispin in 1867, just after the end of the Civil War. By 1870 it had some fifty thousand members, making it the biggest workers' union in the country. Nine years later the group began admitting women; by 1886 they made up 10 percent of its membership. However, the Knights of Crispin remained a regional organization serving only the northeastern sector of the nation. Also, it was poorly organized. So it declined and faded from view in the 1890s.

More national in scope and influence, as well as better organized, was the Knights of Labor, established in 1869. By 1886 it boasted a membership of more than seven hundred thousand. The group staged a number of large-scale strikes against major industries. In the 1880s it successfully won concessions from two of the largest U.S. railroad companies (the Union Pacific and infamous robber baron Jay Gould's Wabash Railroad). Just as it seemed to be hitting its stride, however, the Knights of Labor went into decline. This was partly because its leaders mismanaged a number of negotiations with factory owners and also because the group was unfairly linked in the public eye to violence that marred a major strike in Chicago. By the 1890s the group had lost most of its members and influence.

Many of those who left the Knights joined an up-and-coming labor organization called the American Federation of Labor (AFL). It was established in the 1880s by Samuel Gompers (1850–1924), a Dutch-born American who, as a young man, had worked in the cigar-making industry.

The AFL was a sort of umbrella organization. Effectively exploiting the concept of strength in numbers, it coordinated the efforts of numerous regional and local unions, giving it considerable clout. Gompers and his assistants concentrated most of their energies in two areas. One was collective bargaining, in which industrial and other workers sat down with their employers, negotiated, and drew up new contracts. The AFL also lobbied state and federal lawmakers to enact new legislation designed to alleviate the plight of workers. (A later, similar umbrella labor organization, the Congress of Industrial Organizations, or CIO, eventually merged with the AFL, creating the highly influential AFL-CIO.)

In arguing and negotiating with industrialists and other bosses, AFL representatives urged them to be realistic and practical. Sooner or later, they said, workers would become fed up with unfair, unsafe working conditions and go on strike, costing the company money and damaging its image. Gompers summed it up this way:

The individual working men accept conditions as they are, until driven to desperation. Then they throw

Labor leader Samuel Gompers established the American Federation of Labor (AFL) in the 1880s.

down their tools and strike. . . . Let no man fool himself. When in sheer desperation, driven to the last, where they can no longer submit to the lording of the master, they strike, they quit, and all the pent up anger gives vent in fury.[55]

It would be better for everyone involved, Gompers stressed, to avoid such costly incidents by crafting mutually beneficial bargains.

Several other successful large organizations that sought to improve the lot of industrial workers rose to prominence

African Americans Form a Union

During the Industrial Revolution, African Americans, then still an oppressed minority, were accepted in a few white-run unions but were excluded from most others. The first successful African American–run labor organization was the Brotherhood of Sleeping Car Porters, established in 1925. Its members worked as baggage handlers, ticket takers, and other jobs on passenger trains across the nation. At the time the union appeared, more than twenty thousand black Americans filled these positions. At first, the Pullman Company, which ran most of the passenger trains, discouraged the porters from forming a union because it wanted to avoid raising their pay. So a group of porters asked a prominent African American, A. Philip Randolph, to organize the union. For a while, the group had little or no success in dealing with the Pullman management. But in 1936 the American Federation of Labor recognized the Brotherhood and this led to a contract with Pullman, which included a pay raise a year later. As the first contract between an American company and a black union, it was historic.

The Brotherhood of Sleeping Car Porters (BSCP) was the first successful African American–run labor organization.

in the 1890s and the two decades that followed. Among the more successful was the United Mine Workers (UMW). One key to that success was an inclusive, unprejudiced membership policy that welcomed African Americans and eastern European immigrants, even those who spoke no English. (In contrast, the AFL at first excluded blacks, unskilled immigrants, and women.)

In 1902 the UMW organized a strike against the coal industry in Pennsylvania in which one hundred thousand miners walked off the job. At first the mine owners refused to negotiate. But then President Theodore Roosevelt stepped in and helped to put together a deal between the two sides. The miners returned to work with a 10 percent pay raise and shorter work days.

The Struggle Pays Off

The results of the 1902 UMW strike were a clear victory for organized labor. Overall, however, few unions and strikes during that period were as successful as this one. More often negotiations with employers and workers' strikes achieved only partial success or none at all. Moreover, there were frequent outbreaks of violence during strikes, which worsened the already strained relations between workers and industry.

One of the most dramatic and widely publicized of these violent episodes was the infamous Haymarket Square riot, which took place on May 4, 1886, in Chicago. The day before the riot, there had been a meeting of workers who had gone on strike against a local harvesting-machine company. Tempers had flared, and police had fired on the crowd, killing six workers. On May 4, as a huge crowd gathered in Haymarket Square to protest the deaths, someone threw a bomb at the police, and the crowd erupted into chaos. Seven policemen and at least four civilians died.

The Haymarket affair had a negative impact on the efforts of organized labor. For several years, industrialists, police, and government officials used the riot (which they blamed on the workers) as an excuse to suppress or refuse to deal with unions. The Knights of Labor was one of the chief casualties. Though it was not involved in the incident, public rumors to the contrary ruined its reputation.

However, union organizers and the rank and file of several growing unions persevered. In the decades that followed they slowly but steadily gained economic and political power and influence that forced industry to change. In 1905 the Industrial Workers of the World (IWW) was established in Chicago. Its willingness to include women and members of all races and nationalities made it widely popular among industrial workers. The IWW staged many strikes, some of which were successful. Another victory for labor occurred in 1912 when Massachusetts became the first U.S. state to mandate a minimum wage for women and children. The following year the federal government recognized the growing power of organized labor and formed the Department of Labor, which was charged with helping to settle major labor disputes in the country.

Several other milestones in industrial workers' long struggle for fair pay and treatment involved the railroad industry. In 1916, after a group of unions threatened a nationwide railway strike that would have brought much of the economy to a halt, railroad workers were granted an eight-hour workday. In 1926 Congress passed the Railway Labor Act. It forced the railroads to bargain with their employees who had grievances, and barred those companies from discriminating against workers who joined unions.

A major culmination of these and other gains made by organized labor in the closing years of the Industrial Revolution was the 1935 Wagner Act (or National Labor Relations Act). It was the first federal legislation to protect the rights of all U.S. workers to organize into unions. It also gave unions the right to elect representatives to bargain with employers. Some influential individuals challenged the legality of this law. But in 1937 the U.S. Supreme Court upheld it.

The reputation of labor unions was hurt by the Haymarket Square riot in Chicago after a bomb was thrown into a group of policemen, killing at least eleven people.

Strikers and Their Children Are Beaten

Many labor strikes against factories resulted in violent clashes between workers, police, and sometimes security guards or thugs who worked for the factory owners. A particularly violent incident took place in 1912 in Lawrence, Massachusetts, where textile workers were protesting recent wage cuts. One of the organizers of the strikers, Elizabeth G. Flynn, later described the mayhem that occurred when, unprovoked, police suddenly attacked strikers and their children who were trying to board a train:

Just as they were ready to board the train, they were surrounded by police. Troopers surrounded the station outside to keep others out. Children were clubbed and torn away from their parents and a wild scene of brutal disorder took place. Thirty-five frantic women and children were arrested, thrown screaming and fighting into patrol wagons. They were beaten into submission and taken to the police station. . . . It was a day without parallel in American labor history.

Elizabeth G. Flynn, *The Rebel Girl: An Autobiography.* New York: International, 1973, p. 128.

In that same year, two more enormous victories for industrial workers occurred. First, the giant automaker General Motors agreed to deal with the United Auto Workers (a union affiliated with the CIO). Second, the U.S. Steel Company negotiated with a major steel workers' union and granted its employees a 10 percent pay raise and a forty-hour workweek.

At that historic moment, many of those who benefited, though thankful, no longer remembered the struggles of preceding generations of industrial workers. As the Industrial Revolution began to morph into the technological age, most people looked forward rather than backward. Yet the truth was that the many ordinary workers who entered the middle class during the mid-twentieth century stood on the shoulders of millions of less fortunate workers who had come before them. The laborers of the great age of machines had displayed courage and tenacity in the face of poverty and hardship, hoping that their children and grandchildren might enjoy better lives. And those efforts had not been in vain.

Notes

Introduction: Life Before the Industrial Revolution

1. Laura L. Frader, *The Industrial Revolution: A History in Documents*. New York: Oxford University Press, 2006, pp. 20–21.
2. Frader, *The Industrial Revolution*, p. 20.
3. Peter Gaskell, *Artisans and Machinery*. London: John W. Parker, 1836, pp. 11–16.
4. Encarta, "The Industrial Revolution: Costs and Benefits." http://encarta.msn.com/encyclopedia_761577952_5/Industrial_Revolution.html#s24.

Chapter One: Life in the Industrial Towns

5. Quoted in Erna O. Hellerstein et al., eds., *Victorian Women: A Documentary Account of Women's Lives in Nineteenth-Century England, France, and the United States*. Palo Alto, CA: Stanford University Press, 1981, pp. 296–300.
6. Frader, *The Industrial Revolution*, p. 75.
7. Jacob A. Riis, *How the Other Half Lives: Studies Among the Tenements of New York*. New York: Scribner's, 1907, pp. 8–9.
8. Quoted in Sidney Pollard and Colin Holmes, eds., *Documents of European Economic History: The Process of Industrialization, 1750–1870*. New York: St. Martin's, 1968, pp. 494–95.
9. Quoted in Cotton Times, "Understanding the Industrial Revolution: Slum Housing." www.cottontimes.co.uk/housingo.htm.
10. History Learning Site, "Diseases in Industrial Cities in the Industrial Revolution." www.historylearningsite.co.uk/diseases_industrial_revolut.htm.
11. Friedrich Engels, *The Condition of the Working Classes in England*. London: Panther, 1969, pp. 172–73.
12. Lady Bell, *At the Works: A Study of a Manufacturing Town*. London: Thomas Nelson, 1911, p. 124.
13. Frader, *The Industrial Revolution*, p. 92.
14. Arthur G. Nikelly, "Alcoholism: Social as Well as Psycho-Medical Problem—the Missing 'Big Picture.'" www.unhooked.com/sep/bigpict.htm.

Chapter Two: Conditions in Industrial Workplaces

15. Quoted in *New York Times*, April 6, 1912, p. 14.
16. Quoted in Norman Ware, *The Industrial Worker, 1840–1860: The Reaction*

of American Industrial Society to the Advance of the Industrial Revolution. Chicago: I.R. Dee, 1990, p. 50.

17. Quoted in Ware, The Industrial Worker, 1840–1860, p. 33.

18. Edgar Murphy, Problems of the Present South. New York: Macmillan, 1904, p. 38.

19. Quoted in Richard L. Tames, ed., Documents of the Industrial Revolution, 1750–1850. London: Hutchinson, 1971, pp. 90–91.

20. Quoted in Laura Del Col, "The Life of the Industrial Worker in Nineteenth-Century England," Victorian Web. www.victorianweb.org/history/workers2.html.

21. Andrew Roy, The Coal Mines. Cleveland: Robinson, Savage, 1876, pp. 134–35.

22. Quoted in Leon Stein, ed., Out of the Sweatshop: The Struggle for Industrial Democracy. New York: Quadrangle, 1977, pp. 188, 192; also available at William G. Shepherd, "Eyewitness at the Triangle," The Triangle Factory Fire. www.ilr.cornell.edu/trianglefire/texts/stein_ootss/ootss_wgs.html?location=Fire.

23. Riis, How the Other Half Lives, pp. 122–25.

24. Quoted in Stein, ed., Out of the Sweatshop, p. 60.

Chapter Three: Women Who Worked in Industry

25. Quoted in Frader, The Industrial Revolution, p. 129.

26. Quoted in Frader, The Industrial Revolution, p. 131.

27. Barbara M. Wertheimer, We Were There: The Story of Working Women in America. New York: Pantheon, 1997, p. 63.

28. Quoted in Internet Modern History Source Book, "Harriet Robinson: Lowell Mill Girls." www.fordham.edu/halsall/mod/robinson-lowell.html.

29. Quoted in Internet Modern History Source Book, "Harriet Robinson."

30. Riis, How the Other Half Lives, p. 240.

31. Quoted in John D. Andrews and W.D.P. Bliss, History of Women in Trade Unions. New York: Arno, 1974, p. 100.

32. Riis, How the Other Half Lives, p. 236.

33. Quoted in Ware, The Industrial Worker, p. 77.

34. Quoted in Helen Sumner, History of Women in Industry in the United States. New York: Arno Press, 1974, p. 102.

35. Quoted in Sumner, History of Women in Industry in the United States, p. 22.

Chapter Four: Child Labor in Industry

36. Quoted in Samuel Slater: Father of the American Industrial Revolution, "Child Labor." www.woonsocket.org/slaterchildlabor.

37. Michael Thomas Sadler, Memoirs of the Life and Writings of Michael Thomas Sadler. London: R.B. Seeley, 1842, p. 347.

38. Quoted in Spartacus Educational: The Industrial Revolution, "Working Hours in Factories." www.spartacus.schoolnet.co.uk/IRtime.htm.

39. Quoted in Spartacus Educational, "Working Hours in Factories."
40. Quoted in Spartacus Educational: The Industrial Revolution, "Interview with David Bywater." www.spartacus.schoolnet.co.uk/IRbywater.htm.
41. Quoted in Spartacus Educational: The Industrial Revolution, "Physical Deformities." www.spartacus.schoolnet.co.uk/IRdeformities.htm.
42. Spartacus Educational: The Industrial Revolution, "Interview with Hannah Brown." www.spartacus.schoolnet.co.uk/IRbrown.htm.
43. Quoted in Spartacus Educational: The Industrial Revolution, "Factory Accidents." www.spartacus.schoolnet.co.uk/IRaccidents.htm.
44. Quoted in Spartacus Educational: The Industrial Revolution, "Punishment in Factories." www.spartacus.schoolnet.co.uk/IRpunishments.htm.
45. Quoted in Spartacus Educational, "Punishment in Factories."
46. Quoted in Spartacus Educational: The Industrial Revolution, "Interview with John Birley." www.spartacus.schoolnet.co.uk/IRbirley.htm.
47. Quoted in Spartacus Educational: The Industrial Revolution, "Interview with Robert Blincoe." www.spartacus.schoolnet.co.uk/IRblincoe.htm.

Chapter Five: Immigrant Industrial Workers

48. Quoted in Internet Modern History Source Book, "What Is an American?" www.fordham.edu/halsall/mod/crevecour2.html.
49. Riis, *How the Other Half Lives,* p. 21.
50. Quoted in Baltimore Literary Heritage Project, "Ottmar Mergenthaler." http://baltimoreauthors.ubalt.edu/writers/ottomergenthaler.htm.
51. Sukkoo Kim, "Immigration, Industrial Revolution, and Urban Growth in the United States, 1820–1920." www.economics.uci.edu/docs/THD%20workshop/sp08/kim.pdf.
52. Walter Lippmann, *Drift and Mastery.* New York: M. Kennerley, 1914, p. 211.

Chapter Six: Organized Labor and Industry

53. Quoted in Spartacus Educational: Trade Union Movement, "Knights of Labor." www.spartacus.schoolnet.co.uk/USAknights.htm.
54. Quoted in Spartacus Educational, "Knights of Labor."
55. Quoted in Spartacus Educational: Trade Union Movement, "Samuel Gompers." www.spartacus.schoolnet.co.uk/USAgompers.htm.

Time Line

1752
American inventor Benjamin Franklin shows that lightning is a form of electricity.

1756
The Seven Years' War begins with fighting on three different continents—Asia, Europe, and North America.

1765
The introduction of the spinning jenny begins to revolutionize the textile industry.

1776
England's thirteen American colonies declare their independence.

1791
Thomas Paine publishes *The Rights of Man*.

1800
The Library of Congress is established with a budget of five thousand dollars to purchase some nine hundred books.

1810
In South America, Argentina gains its independence.

1811–1815
In England, the Luddites, workers opposed to industrialization, attack factories.

1832
A committee of Britain's Parliament conducts an investigation into child labor practices.

1836
Samuel F.B. Morse invents the telegraph, an enormous advance in communications.

1842
Labor unions become legal in the United States.

1847
New Hampshire becomes the first U.S. state to mandate a ten-hour workday for industrial workers.

1850
Samuel Gompers, who will later establish the influential American Federation of Labor, is born.

1851
The average wage earned by American industrial workers is seven to ten dollars per week.

1861–1865
The Union and the Confederacy fight the American Civil War.

1865–1890
America receives its second large wave of foreign immigrants, numbering about 10 million people.

1869
A disaster at Pennsylvania's Avondale coal mine kills 110 miners; transcontinental railroad service is established in the United States.

1870–1871
The Franco-Prussian War rocks Europe.

1876
Alexander Graham Bell introduces the telephone.

1881
U.S. president James Garfield is assassinated.

1883
The first skyscraper (rising ten stories) is built in Chicago; the Brooklyn Bridge is inaugurated in New York City.

1902
A labor union, the United Mine Workers, successfully strikes, gaining higher wages and shorter workdays for its members.

1904
The Russo-Japanese War begins as Russia and Japan vie for control of Manchuria and Korea.

1906
An earthquake rocks San Francisco and triggers a fire that lasts for three days and burns more than 4 square miles (10 sq. km) of the city.

1910
An estimated thirty thousand garment sweatshops are in operation in New York City.

1911
The Triangle Shirtwaist factory fire kills 146 workers, shocking Americans and leading to regulations on sweatshops.

1914
World War I erupts in Europe.

1917
The United States joins World War I on the side of the Allies—Great Britain, France, Belgium, Italy, and Russia.

1929
The stock market crash on October 29 triggers the beginning of the Great Depression.

1937
The U.S. Congress passes the Wagner Act, which gives all American workers the right to organize labor unions.

For More Information

Books

T.S. Ashton and Pat Hudson, *The Industrial Revolution, 1760–1830*. New York: Oxford University Press, 1998. This is an excellent general look at the early years of the Industrial Revolution. Hudson, an economic historian, provides commentary updating Ashton's classic 1949 book.

Laura L. Frader, *The Industrial Revolution: A History in Documents*. New York: Oxford University Press, 2006. This is one of the best collections of primary sources for the Industrial Revolution.

Pamela Horn, *Children's Work and Welfare, 1780–1890*. Cambridge, MA: Cambridge University Press, 1995. This book examines child labor during the Industrial Revolution.

Gary J. Kornblith, ed., *The Industrial Revolution in America*. Boston: Houghton Mifflin, 1998. This well-written book explains how the United States became an industrial giant.

Charles More, *Understanding the Industrial Revolution*. London: Routledge, 2000. This clearly written volume makes the Industrial Revolution accessible to nonscholars.

Clark Nardinelli, *Child Labor and the Industrial Revolution*. Bloomington: Indiana University Press, 1990. This work contains much useful information about what child laborers experienced in factories.

Tracee Sioux, *Immigration, Migration, and the Industrial Revolution*. New York: Rosen, 2004. The author discusses the role of immigration and immigrants during the machine age.

Richard L. Tames, *Life During the Industrial Revolution*. London: Reader's Digest, 1999. This book offers a clearly written overview of society and living conditions in this crucial era.

Norman Ware, *The Industrial Worker, 1840–1860: The Reaction of American Industrial Society to the Advance of the Industrial Revolution*. Chicago: I.R. Dee, 1990. This work offers a detailed examination of how emerging industries and the factory system affected American workers.

Barbara M. Wertheimer, *We Were There: The Story of Working Women in America*. New York: Pantheon, 1997. The author presents an informative study of women workers, their work conditions, and their labor organizations, including those of the Industrial Revolution period.

Adam Woog, *A Sweatshop During the Industrial Revolution*. San Diego: Lucent, 2002. This book provides much useful information about the many sweatshops spawned by the Industrial Revolution.

Susan Zlotnick, *Women, Writing, and the Industrial Revolution*. Baltimore: Johns Hopkins University Press, 2001. This work is an original and valuable study of women workers and writers and their contributions to the Industrial Revolution.

Web Sites

American History 102 (http://us.history.wisc.edu/hist102/lectures/lecture08.html). This Web site by history professor Stanley K. Schultz offers the reader-friendly lecture "Foreign Immigrants in Industrial America," which is a good introduction to the issue of immigration during the nineteenth-century industrial age.

History Learning Site: Industrial Revolution (www.historylearningsite.co.uk/industrial_revolution_towns.htm). This Web site's article "Life in Industrial Towns" is a concise overview of workers' living conditions during the Industrial Revolution.

Internet Modern History Source Book: The Industrial Revolution (www.fordham.edu/halsall/mod/mods book14.html). This very useful collection of articles on the Industrial Revolution includes several on its social, political, and urban effects.

Spartacus Educational: Child Labor (www.spartacus.schoolnet.co.uk/IR child.main.htm). This very useful site presented by historian John Simkin and the Spartacus Educational organization contains loads of information about child labor during the Industrial Revolution, including dozens of eyewitness accounts by workers, overseers, reformers, and others.

The Triangle Factory Fire (http://www.ilr.cornell.edu/trianglefire/narrative1.html). This Web site is a handsomely mounted, multifaceted, accurate, and informative source of information about one of the worst industrial disasters in U.S. history.

The Victorian Web: The Industrial Revolution: An Overview (www.victorianweb.org/technology/ir/irov.html). An excellent compilation of short articles on Industrial Revolution topics, this site includes textiles, railroads, inventors, engineers, a chronology, and much more.

Index

Picture Credits

About the Author

In addition to his acclaimed volumes on the ancient world, historian Don Nardo has written and edited many books for young adults about modern European and American history, including *The Age of Colonialism, The French Revolution, The Atlantic Slave Trade, The Declaration of Independence, The Great Depression,* and *World War II in the Pacific.* Mr. Nardo also writes screenplays and teleplays and composes music. He lives with his wife, Christine, in Massachusetts.